RONALD REAGAN:
A MAN TRUE TO HIS WORD

RONALD REAGAN:

A MAN TRUE
TO HIS WORD

Edited By
James S. Brady

Additional Research
by
Michael P. Hickey

Front Cover Photo: Michael Evans, The White House
Back Cover Photo: Jack Knightlinger, The White House

Library of Congress Catalog Card Number 84-60239

TABLE OF CONTENTS

FOREWORD

On July 17, 1980, Ronald Reagan accepted our Party's nomination as our candidate for the Presidency of the United States. In his acceptance speech, he promised to do whatever necessary in his administration to eliminate sexual discrimination.

During a campaign press conference on October 14, 1980, he promised that "one of the first Supreme Court vacancies in my administration will be filled by the most qualified woman I can find."

On August 7, 1983, President Reagan addressed the Republican Women's Leadership Forum in San Diego. Here's part of what he said:

Just look at the record. For the first time in history, three women serve in the Cabinet of the United States— Secretary Dole, Secretary Heckler, and Ambassador Kirkpatrick.

We've also appointed more women to top policy-making positions in our first two years than any previous Administration has in a similar period. We've appointed more than 1200 women to executive positions throughout the government. And while that record is better than any of our predecessors, it's only a beginning. And, of course, in another beginning, I'm proud to say we appointed the first woman to the Supreme Court.

There's no question that, on the role of women in government, Ronald Reagan has indeed lived up to his campaign promises. In fact, a careful look at the record of his administration in the context of the goals and aims set forth in his 1980 campaign, shows a similar correlation between what was promised and what has been done.

Yet somehow, in the heat of partisan politics, and especially in the heat of political campaigns, facts and records like that seem frequently to become obscured, if not distorted.

It is our hope that this book will help keep the record straight.

But we have carefully avoided the temptation to produce a book that steps into the middle of controversial campaign issues. In fact, with very few exceptions like the above statement on presidential appointments, there is no discussion of Ronald Reagan's performance in the White House.

There are a number of reasons why. Primary, however, is our belief that his performance is reviewed constantly, both by those favorable to him and those unfavorable as well, and that his performance should really be viewed by the American people according to the impact it has made, or failed to make, on their own lives.

But, as Jim Brady reminds us, the man cannot be separated from the President; it is the character of the man that will determine the character of his Presidency.

We feel that Jim Brady has provided us an outstanding vehicle for coming to a deeper understanding of the character of Ronald Reagan. It is that character that led us to select the title, Ronald Reagan: A Man True to His Word.

Because, throughout his political career, he has been true to his word, a fact that is ably and clearly demonstrated in this compilation of those words.

The National Federation of Republican Women is pleased and proud to publish Ronald Reagan: A Man True to His Word. We invite readers to examine it carefully and consider its content in the face of the events and actions that have taken place since Ronald Reagan assumed the Presidency of the United States.

It is our hope that you will come away with a better understanding of Ronald Reagan—the man and the President.

Betty Rendel
President, National Federation
of Republican Women

EDITOR'S NOTE

With very few exceptions, the material in this book has been assembled from speeches and statements that received considerable public exposure and range in length from some of the President's more memorable one-liners to extended passages from some of his major speeches. In addition, the appendix includes certain of his more important speeches in their entirety.

A careful reader will undoubtedly note that some passages appear more than once in the book. This is simply because their content and message make them appropriate for more than one section and to attempt to develop a particular theme without their inclusion would have made that section incomplete.

It was the development of those themes that led to the selection of passages to be included in the book—the quest for world peace, restoration of a sound economy for America to benefit all our citizens, the greatness and indomitable spirit of the American people, concern for the legacy we will leave for future generations, and, of course, examples of Ronald Reagan's delightful sense of humor.

There are several people to whom I am extremely grateful for their assistance in this project: Betty Rendel, President of the National Federation of Republican Women, for creating the concept and asking me to do the book; to the President of the United States, Ronald Reagan, for his constant support and friendship; and most of all, to my wife Sarah, from whose love and encouragement I have been able to draw strength and will that I never realized existed.

James S. Brady

INTRODUCTION

The Great Communicator

Allow me to set the scene for you.

Let's go back 19 years. It's October 27, 1964. Senator Barry Goldwater's campaign against Lyndon Johnson for the Presidency of the United States is badly in need of a boost.

Ronald Reagan, then 53 years of age and known to most Americans only as a movie actor and host of two popular television series, is making a nationally-televised speech on behalf of Senator Goldwater and the Republican Party.

Ronald Reagan is speaking:

You and I have a rendezvous with history. We will preserve for our children this, the last best hope for man on earth, or we will sentence them to take the last step into a thousand years of darkness. If we fail, at least let our children, and our children's children, say of us we justified our brief moment here. We did all that could be done.

The speech was called "A Time for Choosing," and while it did not bring victory for Barry Goldwater, it breathed new life, and new money, into the Republican party.

"A Time for Choosing" raised $1 million for Republican candidates, more than any political speech had ever raised before.

Columnist David Broder called "A Time for Choosing," "the most successful political debut since William Jennings Bryan electrified the 1896 Democratic convention with his 'Cross of Gold' speech. In a half hour of national television, Ronald Reagan has transformed himself from a fading celebrity into the nation's most important conservative politician."

Thus was the image of Ronald Reagan, The Great Communicator, born.

Now let's move forward in time again. 19 years. In fact, 19 years exactly.

It's October 27, 1983. President Ronald Reagan is addressing the nation again on television, this time with the dual subjects of the tragic massacre of our marines in Lebanon and the rescue mission carried out by American forces to secure the safety and release of American citizens held under a shoot-to-kill curfew in Grenada.

In a nationwide survey conducted prior to this address, approximately one half of the American people supported the President's decision to send troops into Grenada.

Even the President's critics are calling his Lebanon and Grenada address perhaps his greatest ever as President. They listen to passages like:

These small peaceful nations needed our help. Three of them don't have armies at all and the others have very limited forces.

The legitimacy of their request plus my own concern for our citizens dictated my decision. I believe our Government has a responsibility to go to the aid of its citizens if their right to life and liberty is threatened. The nightmare of our hostages in Iran must never be repeated.

Following President Reagan's address, a subsequent survey by the same pollsters showed that an overwhelming 80 percent of the American people approved of the President's decision to send American troops into Grenada.

Thus does the image of Ronald Reagan, The Great Communicator, flourish today.

Rarely have we had a president as eloquent, as skilled an orator, as Ronald Reagan.

And because of that, who could better tell the story of Ronald Reagan than the man himself, through his own words?

Putting together a book like this one is a true challenge, not so much the decisions on what to include, but more the decisions on what to exclude.

We have not attempted in choosing the selections to be included in this book to jump into the middle of specific, controversial issues which will receive more than enough coverage throughout any presidential campaign.

Rather, we have opted for selections that help create a portrait of Ronald Reagan, the man and the president.

Knowing Ronald Reagan personally and having had the privilege and pleasure of working closely with him, I realize that the man and the president are inseparable. He is conducting his presidency based on the same fundamental principles that have guided his life.

It is those principles we have attempted to focus on in this book—his compassion and love for all people, for example, and his concern that in recent years we have lost sight of the fact that Government in this country exists to serve those people, not vice versa.

Ronald Reagan is also as devoted to the pursuit of world peace as anyone who has ever lived. He is also, however, pragmatic about the world and times in which we live and realizes that just wishing for world peace is not going to make it happen.

He is also most interested in how Americans of future generations will look back on these years and view the things we accomplish, and fail to accomplish, in our quest to help make their future more secure.

In pursuit of that security, I think Ronald Reagan would be perfectly content to live by those same words he spoke to the American people on October 27, 1964:

"If we fail, at least let our children, and our children's children say of us we justified our brief moment here. We did all that could be done."

CHAPTER 1

"There are no words to express
the extraordinary strength and character
of this breed of people we call Americans."

*One prime reason why Ronald Reagan has never been
afraid to challenge his constituents and others around him
to find solutions to the most difficult problems is his unshakeable conviction that America and the American people are truly special, that they are marked by a character
of greatness and are capable and willing to meet any challenge that confronts them.*

*He believes that our greatness, then, is not necessarily a
greatness of military strength or industrial capability, but
a greatness of spirit that has helped make America unique
among the nations of the world.*

*In his 1964 address in the closing days of Senator Gold-
water's presidential campaign, Ronald Reagan used a story
to remind his audience that what we have here is very
special and must be preserved.*

Not long ago, two friends of mine were talking to a
Cuban refugee. He was a businessman who had escaped
from Castro. In the midst of his tale of horrible experi-
ences, one of my friends turned to the other and said, "We
don't know how lucky we are." The Cuban stopped and
said, "How lucky you are? I had someplace to escape to."
And in that sentence, he told the entire story. If freedom
is lost, there is no place to escape to."

*In his first general election speech during the 1966 Cali-
fornia gubernatorial campaign, Ronald Reagan set a tone
for his campaign that would recur again and again after
his entry into the national political scene.*

We can start a prairie fire that will sweep the nation and
prove that we are number one in more than size and crime
and taxes.

This is a dream, as big and golden as California itself.

In his 1970 re-election campaign in California, Governor Reagan spoke to a group of business and agricultural leaders in Sacramento.

We have never been more prosperous, or more generous with our prosperity, never more truly concerned with the welfare of the less fortunate, with education and equality of opportunity, never more determined to bring decency and order to the world. It is time we ended our obsession with what is wrong and realize how much is right, how great is our power and how little we really have to fear.

Stressing the positive became a Ronald Reagan trademark in his discussions about America. In addition, he addressed the need for his Republican Party and the new conservative movement in America to dedicate their efforts to the preservation and protection of the basic values and principles that he felt had made this nation great in the first place.
In January 1977, he addressed the Intercollegiate Studies Institute and used that theme.

We the members of the new Republican Party believe that the preservation and enhancement of the values that strengthen and protect individual freedom, family life, communities and neighborhoods, and the liberty of our beloved nation should be at the heart of any legislative or political program presented to the American people.

One of Ronald Reagan's favorite descriptions of America is "as a shining city on a hill for all mankind to see." In a 1978 address to the Conservative Political Action Conference Banquet in Washington, D.C., he spoke of America's role in the world and our destiny.

Great nations which fail to meet their responsibilities are consigned to the dustbin of history. We grew from that small, weak republic which had as its assets spirit, optimism, faith in God and an unshakeable belief that free men and women could govern themselves wisely. We became the leader of the free world, an example for all those who cherish freedom. If we are to continue to be that example—if we are to preserve our own freedom, we must shoulder our burden with our eyes fixed on the future, but recognizing the realities of today, not counting on mere hope or wishes. We must be willing to carry out our responsibility as the custodian of individual freedom. Then we will achieve our destiny as a shining city on a hill for all mankind to see.

In 1979, Ronald Reagan announced his candidacy for the Republican nomination for President to a crowd gathered in the New York Hilton. One of the most moving sections of his address dealt with his view of America.

I'm sure that each of us has seen our country from a number of different viewpoints depending on where we've lived and what we've done. For me it has been as a boy growing up in several small towns in Illinois. As a young man in Iowa trying to get a start in the years of the Great Depression and later in California for most of my adult life. I've seen America from the stadium press box as a sportscaster, as an actor, officer of my labor union, soldier, office holder, and as both Democrat and Republican. I've lived in an America where those who often had too little to eat outnumbered those who had enough. There have been four wars in my lifetime and I've seen our country face financial ruin in the Depression. I have also seen the great strength of this nation as it pulled itself up from that ruin to become the dominant force in the world.

Ronald Reagan has perhaps never been more eloquent on America's greatness than when he accepted his party's nomination as their presidential candidate in Detroit, July 17, 1980.

They (the Democratic Party leadership) say that the United States has had its day in the sun, that our nation has passed its zenith. They expect you to tell your children that the American people no longer have the will to cope with their problems; that the future will be one of sacrifice and few opportunities.

My fellow citizens, I utterly reject that view. The American people, the most generous on earth, who created the highest standard of living, are not going to accept the notion that we can only make a better world for others by moving backward ourselves. And those who believe we can have no business leading this nation.

The United States of America is unique in world history because it has a genius for leaders—many leaders—on many levels.

Three-hundred-and-sixty years ago, in 1620, a group of families dared to cross a mighty ocean to build a future for themselves in a new world. When they arrived at Plymouth, Massachusetts, they formed what is called a "compact," an agreement among themselves to build a community and abide by its laws.

This single act—the voluntary binding together of free people to live under the law—set the pattern for what was to come.

A century and a half later, the descendants of those people pledged their lives, their fortunes and their sacred honor to found this nation. Some forfeited their fortunes and their lives; none sacrificed honor.

Four score and seven years later, Abraham Lincoln called upon the people of all America to renew their dedication and their commitment to a government of, for and by the people.

Isn't it once again time to renew our compact of freedom; to pledge to each other all that is best in our lives; all that gives meaning to them—for the sake of this, our beloved and blessed land?

Let us pledge to restore in our time, the American spirit of voluntary service, of cooperation, of private and community initiative; a spirit that flows like a deep and mighty river through the history of our nation.

It is impossible to capture in words the splendor of this vast continent which God has granted as our portion of His creation. There are no words to express the extraordinary strength and character of this breed of people we call Americans.

Everywhere we've met thousands of Democrats, Independents and Republicans from all economic conditions, walks of life, bound together in that community of shared values of family, work, neighborhood, peace and freedom. They are concerned, yes, they're not frightened. They're disturbed but not dismayed. They are the kind of men and women Tom Paine had in mind when he wrote, during the darkest days of the American Revolution, "We have it in our power to begin the world over again."

I ask you not simply to "trust me," but to trust your values—our values—and to hold me responsible for living up to them. I ask you to trust that American spirit which knows no ethnic, religious, social, political, regional or economic boundaries; the spirit that burned with zeal in the hearts of millions of immigrants from every corner of the earth who came here in search of freedom.

Some say that spirit no longer exists. But I've seen it—I've felt it—all across the land, in the big cities, the small towns and in rural America. It's still there, ready to blaze into life if you and I are willing to do what has to be done; we have to do the practical things, the down-to-earth things, such as creating policies that will stimulate our economy, increase productivity and put America back to work.

Can we doubt that only a Divine Providence placed this land, this island of freedom, here as a refuge for all those people in the world who yearn to breathe free? Jews and Christians enduring persecution behind the Iron Curtain; the boat people of Southeast Asia, Cuba and Haiti; the victims of drought and famine in Africa, the freedom fighters in Afghanistan, and our own countrymen held in savage captivity.

I'll confess that I've been a little afraid to suggest what I'm going to suggest. I'm more afraid not to. Can we begin our crusade joined together in a moment of silent prayer? God bless America.

On the eve of the election, in "A Vision for America," Ronald Reagan again challenged those who would dare suggest that the days of America's greatness were past.

Does history still have a place for America, for her people, for her great ideals? There are some who answer "no," that our energy is spent, our days of greatness at an end, that a great national malaise is upon us . . . I find no national malaise. I find nothing wrong with the American people.

Any nation that sees softness in our prosperity or disunity . . . let them understand that we will put aside in a moment the fruits of our prosperity and the luxury of our disagreements if the cause is a safe and peaceful future for our children.

And in his Inaugural Address, President Reagan reminded the American people that we must not dream only small dreams, but rather heroic ones.

They (economic difficulties) will go away because we as Americans have the capacity now, as we have had in the past, to do whatever needs to be done to preserve this last and greatest bastion of freedom.

If we look to the answer as to why for so many years we achieved so much, prospered as no other people on earth, it was because here in this land we unleashed the energy and individual genius of man to a greater extent than has ever been done before.

Freedom and dignity of the individual have been more available and assured here than in any other place on earth. The price for this freedom at times has been high, but we have never been unwilling to pay that price.

It is time for us to realize that we are too great a nation to limit ourselves to small dreams. We're not, as some would have us believe, doomed to an inevitable decline. I do not believe in a fate that will fall on us no matter what we do. I do believe in a fate that will fall on us if we do nothing.

So, with all the creative energy at our command, let us begin an era of national renewal. Let us renew our determination, our courage, and our strength. And let us renew our faith and hope. We have every right to dream heroic dreams.

In an address to a joint session of Congress to present "Our Economic Recovery Program," April 28, 1981, President Reagan used the space shuttle and Carl Sandburg to emphasize again the greatness, the uniqueness of America.

The space shuttle did more than prove our technological capabilities, it raised our expectations once more; it started us dreaming again. The poet Carl Sandburg wrote:

"The Republic is a dream. Nothing happens unless first a dream."

And that's what makes us as Americans different. We've always reached for a new spirit and aimed at a higher goal. We've been courageous and determined, unafraid and bold. Who among us wants to be the first to say that we no longer have those qualities? That we must limp along, doing the same things that have brought us to our present misery. I believe that the people you and I represent are ready to chart a new course. They look to us to meet the great challenge—to reach beyond the commonplace and not fall short for lack of creativity or courage. Someone you know has said he would have nothing to do with thorns must never attempt to gather flowers.

As Carl Sandburg said, all we need to begin with is a dream that we can do better than before.

All we need to have is faith and that dream will come through.

All we need to do is act, and the time for action is now.

A month later, he told the graduating class at the United States Military Academy that he saw progress, that he saw the American people returning to a positive frame of mind.

There is a spiritual revival going on in this country, a hunger on the part of the people to once again be proud of America, all that it is and all that it can be.

The era of self-doubt is over. We've stopped looking at our warts and rediscovered how much there is to love in this blessed land.

In July, 1981, in a message to the American people discussing his tax cut proposals, President Reagan reminded all Americans that the source of our strength, our ability to overcome difficulties, rests in the audience he was addressing.

I have not taken your time this evening merely to ask you to trust me. Instead, I ask you to trust yourselves. Our struggle for nationhood, our unrelenting fight for freedom, our very existence—these have all rested on the assurance that you must be free to shape your life as you are best able to—that no one can stop you from reaching higher or take from you the creativity that has made America the envy of mankind.

President Reagan was aware that much of what he wanted to accomplish in his economic recovery program was dependent not only on the support of the American people, but their willingness to resume a larger role in the effort to provide help and assistance for their fellow citizens in need. In September, 1981, he addressed the American people and challenged them to do just that, and to revive the spirit of volunteerism throughout our land.

I believe the spirit of volunteerism still lives in America. We see examples of it on every hand—the community charity drive, support of hospitals and all manner of non-profit institutions, the rallying around when disaster or tragedy strikes.

The truth is we've let Government take away many things we once considered were really ours to do voluntarily out of the goodness of our hearts and a sense of community pride and neighborliness.

I believe many of you want to do those things again, want to be involved if only someone will ask you or offer the opportunity. Well, we intend to make that offer.

We are launching a nationwide effort to encourage our citizens to join with us in finding where need exists and then to organize volunteer programs to meet that need.

We have already set the wheels of such a volunteer effort in motion.

As Tom Paine said 200 years ago: "We have it within our power to begin the world over again."

What are we waiting for?

In President Reagan's first State of the Union Message, in January of 1982, he used examples from recent American history, examples of heroism, to again show that the true American spirit is indeed alive and well.

In the face of a climate of falsehood and misinformation, we've promised the world a season of truth—the truth of our great civilized ideas: individual liberty, representative government, the rule of law under God.

We've never needed walls, or mine fields or barbwire to keep our people in. Nor do we declare martial law to keep our people from voting for the kind of Government they want.

We speak with pride and admiration of that little band of Americans who overcame insuperable odds to set this nation on course 200 years ago. But our glory didn't end with them—Americans ever since have emulated their deeds.

We don't have to turn to our history books for heroes. They're all around us. One who sits among you here tonight epitomized that heroism at the end of the longest imprisonment ever inflicted on men of our armed forces. Who will ever forget that night when we waited for television to bring us the scene of that first plane landing at Clark Field in the Philippines—bringing our P.O.W.s home. The plane door opened and Jeremiah Denton came slowly down the ramp. He caught sight of our flag, saluted it, said, "God Bless America," and then thanked us for bringing him home.

Just two weeks ago, in the midst of a terrible tragedy on the Potomac, we saw again the spirit of American heroism at its finest—the heroism of dedicated rescue workers saving crash victims from icy waters. And we saw the heroism of one of our young government employees, Lenny Skutnik, who, when he saw a woman lose her grip on the helicopter line, dived into the water and dragged her to safety.

And then there are the countless, quiet, everyday heroes of American life—parents who sacrifice long and hard so their children will know a better life than they've known; church and civic volunteers who help to feed, clothe, nurse and teach the needy; millions who've made our nation, and our nation's destiny, so very special—unsung heroes who may not have realized their own dreams themselves but then who reinvest those dreams in their children.

Don't let anyone tell us that America's best days are behind her—that the American spirit has been vanquished. We've seen it triumph too often in our lives to stop believing in it now.

On April 29, 1982, President Reagan again went before the American people on the Budget Problem. And again, he called them to reach into that reserve, that fortitude that has pulled this nation through so many times before.

Time and again, the American people—you—have worked wonders that have astounded the world. We've done it in war and peace, in good times and bad. Because we're a people who care and who know how to pull together—family by family, community by community, coast to coast—to change things for the better.

The success story of America is neighbor helping neighbor. So tonight, I ask for your help, your voice at this turning point. So often in history, great causes have been won or lost at the last moment because one side or the other lacked that last reserve of character and stamina, of faith and fortitude to see their way through to success.

Later that year, the President traveled to London and to Bonn. Addressing the British Parliament on June 8, and the West German Parliament the following day, he again touched on the importance of individual freedoms to keep a world safe from tyrannical takeover.

In London:

What I am describing now is a plan and a hope for the long term—the march of freedom and democracy which will leave Marxism-Leninism on the ash heap of history as it has left other tyrannies which stifle the freedom and muzzle the self-expression of the people.

And in Bonn:

Our American Revolution was the first revolution in modern history to be fought for the right of self-government and the guarantee of civil liberties.

Americans speak with the deepest reverence of those founding fathers and first citizens who gave us the freedoms we enjoy today. And even though they lived over 200 years ago, we carry them in our hearts as well as our history books.

His trip abroad to spread the message of world peace and America's commitment to maintaining that peace led to the appearance before the United Nations Second Special Session on Disarmament. He reminded those in attendance that, if America's spirit was less noble, the history of the world would have changed radically.

Our foreign policy, as President Eisenhower once said,

is not difficult to state. We are for peace, first last and always for very simple reasons. We know that only in a peaceful atmosphere, a peace with justice, one in which we can be confident, can America prosper as we have known prosperity in the past, he said.

He said to those who challenge the truth of those words, let me point out that at the end of World War II we were the only undamaged industrial power in the world. Our military supremacy was unquestioned. We had harnessed the atom and had the ability to unleash its destructive force anywhere in the world. In short, we could have achieved world domination but that was contrary to the character of our people.

Instead, we wrote a new chapter in the history of mankind.

We used our power and wealth to rebuild the war-ravaged economies of the world, both east and west, including those nations who had been our enemies.

We took the initiative in creating such international institutions as this United Nations where leaders of good will could come together to build bridges for peace and prosperity.

America has no territorial ambitions.

We occupy no countries, and we have built no walls to lock our people in. Our commitment to self-determination, freedom and peace is the very soul of America. That commitment is as strong today as it ever was.

The United States has fought four wars in my lifetime. In each, we struggled to defend freedom and democracy. We are never the aggressors.

America's strength and, yes, her military power, have been a force for peace, not conquest. For democracy, not despotism. For freedom, not tyranny.

In November, 1982, President Reagan addressed the American people on the subject of Arms Control and the MX Missile. Describing the diligence and effort required to help maintain peace in the world and the irony of having to develop great weapons to help secure that peace, he reminded his audience not to lose sight of our special duty to live up to our destiny.

I've always believed that this land was set aside in an uncommon way, that a divine plan placed this great continent between the oceans to be found by a people from every corner of the earth who had a special love of faith, freedom and peace.

Let us reaffirm America's destiny of goodness and good will. Let us work for peace; and as we do, let us remember the lines of the famous old hymn, "Oh God of Love, Oh King of Peace, make wars throughout the world to cease."

In his 1983 State of the Union Message, President Reagan again devoted a considerable portion of his remarks to the indomitability of the American spirit and the incredible ability of the American people to rise to any occasion, no matter how great the challenge.

The very key to our success has been our ability, foremost among nations, to preserve our lasting values by making change work for us rather than against us.

But, as surely as America's pioneer spirit made us the industrial giant of the 20th century, the same pioneer spirit today is opening up another vast frontier of opportunity—the frontier of high technology. In conquering this frontier, we cannot write off our traditional industries, but we must develop the skills and industries that will make us a pioneer of tomorrow.

America's leadership role in the world came to us because of our own strength and because of the values which guide us as a society: free elections, a free press, freedom of religious choice, free trade unions, and, above all, freedom for the individual and rejection of the arbitrary power of the State. These values are the bedrock of our strength.

The future belongs not to governments and ideologies which oppress their peoples but to democratic systems of self-government which encourage individual initiative and guarantee personal freedom.

A very wise man, Bernard Baruch, once said that America has never forgotten the nobler things that brought her into being and that light her path. Our country is a special place because we Americans have always been sustained, through good times and bad, by a noble vision—a vision not only of what the world around us is today, but of what we, as a free people, can make it be tomorrow.

We are realists; we solve our problems instead of ignoring them, no matter how loud the chorus of despair around us.

But we are also idealists, for it was an ideal that brought our ancestors to these shores from every corner of the world.

Back over the years, citizens like ourselves have gathered within these walls when our nation was threatened; sometimes when its very existence was at stake. Always, with courage and common sense they met the crises of their time and lived to see a stronger, better and more prosperous country.

The present situation is no worse and in fact not as bad as some of those they faced. Time and again, they proved that there is nothing we Americans cannot achieve as free men and women.

But the big story about America today is the way that millions of confident, caring people—those extraordinary "ordinary" Americans who never make the headlines and will never be interviewed—are laying the foundation, not just for recovery from our present problems, but for a better tomorrow for all our people.

From coast to coast, on the job and in classrooms and laboratories, at new construction sites and in churches and community groups, neighbors are helping neighbors. And they've already begun the building, the research, the work and the giving that will make our country great again.

I believe this because I believe in them—in the strength of their hearts and minds, in the commitment each of them brings to our daily lives, be they high or humble. The challenge for us in Government is to be worthy of them — to make Government a help, not a hindrance to our people in the challenging but promising days ahead.

At the Biennial Convention of the National Federation of Republican Women, held in Louisville, Kentucky, President Reagan told those in attendance that the American people were indeed rising to the challenges he had presented them.

I believe with all my heart that America is more prosperous, safe and secure today than three years ago. One word sums up the difference between 1983 and 1980: Hope.

You can feel hope being reborn. You can see confidence rising. You can feel a new spirit of optimism spread across our land. America is going forward again. We are meeting the challenge of improving our schools—a challenge neglected for too many years. Some day soon, we will even welcome God back into America's classrooms. We will explore deeper in space, cross new frontiers of high technology, make new medical breakthroughs—and we'll be doing it for the benefit of our children and our children's children.

CHAPTER 2

"I have known four wars in my lifetime— I don't want to see a fifth."

Throughout the 1980 Presidential campaign and even through the early years of his Presidency, Ronald Reagan's opponents have worked diligently to portray him as a hawk, a man who would undoubtedly plunge the United States into war. Those who still hold that opinion today have obviously not been watching, and they certainly haven't been listening.

When he accepted his Party's nomination on July 17, 1980, Ronald Reagan told all those assembled in Detroit, in no uncertain terms, of his commitment to peace.

Of all the objectives we seek, first and foremost is the establishment of lasting world peace.

And he repeated that commitment throughout the campaign.

I have known four wars in my lifetime—I don't want to see a fifth. I pray that never again will we bleed a generation of young Americans into the sands of island beachheads, the mud of European battlefields, or the rice paddies or jungles of Asia. It is our responsibility to preserve world peace because no one else can do it.

And

There is no reason why people in any part of the world should have to live in permanent fear of war or its specter. I believe the time has come for all nations to act in a responsible spirit that doesn't threaten other states. I believe the time is right to move forward on arms control and the resolution of critical regional disputes at the conference table. Nothing will have a higher priority for me and for the American people over the coming months and years.

And

I have two sons. I have a grandson. I have known four wars in my lifetime and I think like all of you that world peace has got to be the principal theme of this nation.

But his commitment to peace did not end with his election to the Presidency. It only grew stronger.

In June, 1982, President Reagan embarked on a journey for peace. It took him to London, where he addressed the British Parliament on June 8, and to Bonn, where he addressed the West German Parliament the following day.

The climax of the trip, however, came on June 17, when he addressed the United Nations Second Special Session on Disarmament. Excerpts from these speeches appear in several locations in this book and elsewhere in this same section.

There are certain passages, however, that bear moving testimony to President Reagan's commitment to peace, lasting peace, for all the world.

In London:

And I know we all look forward to the day when the only industry of war will be the research of historians.

In Bonn, a day later:

The nuclear threat is a terrible beast. Perhaps the banner carried in one of the nuclear demonstrations here in Germany said it best. The sign read, "I am afraid." I know of no Western leader who doesn't sympathize with that earnest plea. To those who march for peace, my heart is with you. I would be at the head of your parade if I believed marching alone could bring about a more secure world.

Earlier I said the German people had built a remarkable cathedral of democracy. But we still have other work ahead. We must build a cathedral of peace, where nations are safe from war and where people need not fear for their liberties. I've heard the history of the famous cathedral at Cologne—how those beautiful soaring spires miraculously survived the destruction all around them, including part of the church itself.

Let us build a cathedral as the people of Cologne built theirs—with the deepest commitment and determination.

Let us build as they did—not just for ourselves but for the generations beyond. For if we construct our peace properly, it will endure as long as the spires of Cologne.

In addressing the United Nations Disarmament Session a week later, President Reagan reminded those assembled that the United States is, and has always been committed to world peace and suggested that history bears ample proof of that commitment. He invited the other nations of the world to join us in our efforts to secure a permanent peace.

We must not only condemn aggression. We must enforce the dictates of our charter and resume the struggle for world peace.

The record of history is clear. Citizens of the United States resort to force reluctantly and only when they must. Our foreign policy, as President Eisenhower once said, is not difficult to state. We are for peace, first, last and always, for very simple reasons. We know that only in a peaceful atmosphere, a peace with justice, one in which we can be confident, can America prosper as we have known prosperity in the past, he said.

He said to those who challenge the truth of those words, let me point out at the end of World War II, we were the only undamaged industrial power in the world. Our military supremacy was unquestioned. We had harnessed the atom and had the ability to unleash its destructive force anywhere in the world. In short, we could have achieved world domination but that was contrary to the character of our people.

Instead, we wrote a new chapter in the history of mankind.

We used our power and wealth to rebuild the war-ravaged economies of the world, both East and West, including those nations who had been our enemies.

We took the initiative in creating such international institutions as this United Nations where leaders of good will could come together to build bridges for peace and prosperity.

America has no territorial ambitions.

We occupy no countries and have built no walls to lock our people in. Our commitment to self-determination is as strong today as it ever was.

The United States has fought four wars in my lifetime.

In each, we struggled for peace, not conquest. For democracy, not despotism. For freedom, not tyranny.

I have come to this hall to call for international recommitment to the basic tenets of the United Nations Charter, that all members practice tolerance and live together in peace as good neighbors under the rule of law forsaking armed force as a means of settling disputes between nations.

What a better world it would be if the guns were silenced, if neighbor no longer encroached on neighbor and all peoples were free to reap the rewards of their toil and determine their own destiny and system of government whatever their choice.

In an address to the American people on November 22, 1982, President Reagan reminded us once again:

This nation's objective has always been to maintain peace by preventing war.

And, in a most important address on March 23, 1983, in which he was to propose an alternative defense system for America, President Reagan stated his belief that:

The human spirit must be capable of rising above dealing with other nations and human beings by threatening their existence.

True concern over the possibility of nuclear destruction has been a recurring theme in a number of Ronald Reagan's addresses. In a commencement ceremony at his alma mater, Eureka College, in May, 1982:

In our 1931 "Prism" we quoted Carl Sandburg, who in his own beautiful way quoted the Mother Prairie, saying, "Have you seen a red sunset dip over one of my cornfields, the shore of night stars, the wave lines of dawn up a wheat valley?" What an idyllic scene that paints in our minds—and what a nightmarish prospect that a huge mushroom cloud might someday destroy such beauty. My duty as President is to ensure that the ultimate nightmare never occurs, that the prairies and the cities and the people who inhabit them remain free and untouched by nuclear conflict.

CHAPTER 3

"We live in a world that's torn by a
great moral struggle—between democracy
and its enemies, between the spirit
of freedom and those who fear freedom."

*While President Reagan has made the pursuit of world
peace his primary goal, he has never lost sight of the fact
that there are those in the world today to whom peace is not
such a precious commodity—especially if it interferes with
their own expansionist ambitions.*

*Even in 1964, in "A Time for Choosing," Ronald Reagan
warned a nation of the dangers that exist to threaten our
freedom, our way of life.*

We are at war with the most dangerous enemy that has
ever faced mankind in his long climb from the swamps to
the stars, and it has been said if we lose that war, and in
so doing, lose this way of freedom of ours, history will
record with the greatest astonishment that those who had
the most to lose did the least to prevent its happening.

*Ronald Reagan has also made it quite clear over the
years that there is no doubt in his mind as to who is the
biggest threat to the security and freedom of America and
the Free World—the Soviet Union. He has steadfastly
maintained that Soviet actions were far more important
than Soviet promises.*

*In an address to his alma mater, Eureka College, he
reminded his audience:*

Standing in the Athenian marketplace 2,000 years ago,
Demosthenes said, "What sane man would let another
man's words rather than his deeds proclaim who is at
peace and who is at war with us?"

*He cited numerous examples of Soviet duplicity during
the 1980 campaign.*

Where is the Soviet restraint promised in the Code of
Détente of 1972? Is it visible in the Russian military build-

up in North Korea? Or in the occupied islands of Japan? Did we see it in Hanoi's annexation of Indochina? In Soviet complicity in the starvation of the people of Cambodia? The Soviet provision of poison gas used against the hill tribesmen of Laos? Is Russian restraint evident in their military intervention with Cuban proxies in wars in Angola and Ethiopia? Is it visible in their imperial invasion of the then independent, neutral nation of Afghanistan, where they executed their own puppet president and his entire family, including even his three-year-old daughter?

Shortly after he took office, President Reagan twice within a week dealt with the Soviet concept of morality—in terms that would be recalled with a chill following the shooting down of Korean Airlines Flight 007.

The only morality they (the Soviets) recognize is what will further their cause, meaning they reserve unto themselves the right to commit any crime, to lie, to cheat.

And, a week later:

They don't subscribe to our sense of morality; they don't believe in an afterlife; they don't believe in a God or a religion. And the only morality they recognize, therefore, is what will advance the cause of socialism.

During the commencement address at Eureka College, President Reagan also dealt with the question of the Soviet Union and its impact on the pursuit of world peace.

How should we deal with the Soviet Union in the years ahead? What framework should guide our conduct and policies toward it? What can we realistically expect from a world power of such deep fears, hostilities and external ambitions?

The Soviet Union is a huge empire ruled by an elite that holds all power and all privilege. They hold it tightly because—as we have seen in Poland—they fear what might happen if even the smallest amount of control slips from their grasp.

But in the midst of social and economic problems, the Soviet dictatorship has forged the largest armed force in the world. It has done so by pre-empting the human needs

of its people and, in the end, this course will undermine the
foundations of the Soviet system.

The Soviet Union continues to support Vietnam in its
occupation of Kampuchea and its massive military presence in Laos. It is engaged in a war of aggression against
Afghanistan. Soviet proxy forces have brought instability
and conflict to Africa and Central America.

*During his June 1982 visits to London, Bonn and then
to the United Nations, President Reagan reminded his
audiences that Russian statements are frequently con-
tradicted by Russian actions, and invited comparison with
the actions of the West.*

In London:

Historians looking back at our time will note the consistent restraint and peaceful intentions of the West. They
will note that it was the democracies who refused to use
the threat of their nuclear monopoly in the 40's and early
50's for territorial or imperial gain. Had that monopoly
been in the hands of the Communist world, the map of
Europe, indeed, the world, would look very different today.
And certainly they will note it was not the democracies
that invaded Afghanistan or suppressed Polish Solidarity
or used chemical and toxin warfare in Afghanistan or
Southeast Asia.

*In Bonn the following day, he reminded the West Ger-
man Parliament:*

We cannot simply assume every nation wants the peace
we so earnestly desire. The Polish people would tell us
there are those who would use military force to repress
others who want only basic human rights. The freedom
fighters of Afghanistan would tell us as well that the
threat of aggression has not receded from the world.

*And when President Reagan addressed the United Na-
tions Second Special Disarmament Session a week later,
having already reminded those in attendance of the record
of the United States in pursuing world peace, he invited
comparison to the record of the Soviet Union.*

Since World War II, the record of tyranny has included
Soviet violation of the Yalta agreements leading to domi-

nation of Eastern Europe, symbolized by the Berlin Wall, a grim, gray monument to repression that I visited just a week ago. It includes the takeovers of Czechoslovakia, Hungary and Afghanistan and the ruthless repression of the proud people of Poland.

Soviet-sponsored guerillas and terrorists are at work in Central and South America, in Africa, the Middle East, in the Caribbean and in Europe, violating human rights and unnerving the world with violence. Communist atrocities in Southeast Asia, Afghanistan and elsewhere continue to shock the free world as refugees escape to tell of their horror.

The decade of so-called detente witnessed the most massive Soviet buildup of military power in history.

In his March 23, 1983 televised address to the American people in which he proposed a new defense system, the President reminded us that Soviet threats are not limited to other nations, but affect the United States as well.

As the Soviets have increased their military power, they have been emboldened to extend that power. They are spreading their military influence in ways that can directly challenge our vital interests and those of our allies.

The final fact is that the Soviet Union is acquiring what can only be considered as an offensive military force. They have continued to build far more intercontinental ballistic missiles than they could possibly need to deter an attack. Their conventional forces are trained and equipped not so much to defend against an attack as they are to permit sudden, surprise offensives of their own.

On March 31, 1983, President Reagan addressed the Los Angeles World Affairs Council in Beverly Hills and spoke of the Soviet threat to the very principles on which this nation, and other free nations, are built.

We live in a world in which total war would mean catastrophe. We also live in a world that's torn by a great moral struggle—between democracy and its enemies, between the spirit of freedom and those who fear freedom.

All the moral values which this country cherishes—freedom, democracy, the right of peoples and nations to determine their own destiny, to speak and write, to live and worship as they choose—all these basic rights are fundamentally challenged by a powerful adversary which does not wish these values to survive.

It's interesting to compare a statement made by President Reagan at Eureka College's commencement exercise in May 1982 with a statement he made to the American people after the rescue mission to Grenada in October 1983.

At Eureka he said:

The Soviet Union cannot escape responsibility for the violence and suffering in the region caused by its support for Cuban activities in Central America and its accelerated transfer of advanced military equipment to Cuba.

And, after the Grenadian rescue mission:

Grenada, we were told, was a friendly island paradise for tourism. Well, it wasn't. It was a Soviet-Cuban colony being readied as a major military bastion to export terror and undermine democracy. We got there just in time.

It should also be noted that to President Reagan, the earlier downing of the Korean Airliner by the Soviet Union, while truly a "barbaric act," was nonetheless in keeping with Soviet traditions and history.

While events in Afghanistan and elsewhere have left few illusions about the willingness of the Soviet Union to advance its interests through violence and intimidation, all of us had hoped that certain irreducible standards of civilized behavior nonetheless obtained. But this event shocks the sensibilities of people everywhere.

Where human life is valued, extraordinary efforts are extended to preserve and protect it. Civilized society must ask searching questions about the nature of regimes where such standards do not apply.

What can we think of a regime that so broadly trumpets its vision of peace and global disarmament and yet so callously and quickly commits a terrorist act to sacrifice the lives of innocent human beings?

CHAPTER 4

"... It is sadly ironic that in these modern times,
it still takes weapons to prevent war.
I wish it did not."

Faced with the reality, then, that no matter how determined the United States may be to see a lasting world peace, there are forces in the world equally determined to achieve world domination, Ronald Reagan has steadily maintained the need for a strong America in order to assure that peace. Peace through strength.

In 1977, Ronald Reagan addressed the Intercollegiate Studies Institute at a banquet held in the Mayflower Hotel. He spoke of the need for a new conservative movement in America, one to recognize the inherent rights of all individuals while maintaining America's strength.

The United States must always stand for peace and liberty in the world and for the rights of the individual. Given that there are other nations with potentially hostile design, we recognize that we can reach our goals only while maintaining a superior national defense, second to none.

Just over a year later, Ronald Reagan made similar observations to the Conservative Political Action Conference in Washington, D.C.

America will remain great and act responsibly so long as it exercises power—wisely, and not in the bullying sense —but exercises it nonetheless.

We became the leader of the free world, an example for all those who cherish freedom. If we are to continue to be that example—if we are to preserve our own freedom—we must understand those who would dominate us and deal with them with determination.

In his acceptance speech at the Republican National Convention in Detroit, the new presidential nominee spelled out in clearest terms his determination to keep

America secure from the threat of domination by outside forces.

I do not favor a peacetime draft or registration, but I do favor pay and benefit levels that will attract and keep highly motivated men and women in our volunteer forces and back them up with an active reserve trained and ready for instant call in case of emergency.

It is the responsibility of the President of the United States, in working for peace, to insure that the safety of our people cannot be successfully threatened by a hostile foreign power. As president, fulfilling that responsibility will be my No. 1 priority.

But neither can we be naive or foolish. Four times in my lifetime, America has gone to war, bleeding the lives of its young men into the sands of island beachheads, the fields of Europe and the jungles and rice paddies of Asia. We know only too well that war comes not when the forces of freedom are strong, it is when they are weak that tyrants are tempted.

We simply cannot learn these lessons the hard way again without risking our destruction.

Of all the objectives we seek, first and foremost is the establishment of lasting world peace. We must always stand ready to negotiate in good faith, ready to pursue any reasonable avenue that holds forth the promise of lessening tensions and furthering the prospects of peace. But let our friends and those who may wish us ill take note: the United States has an obligation to its citizens and to the people of the world never to let those who would destroy freedom dictate the future course of life on this planet. I would regard my election as proof that we have renewed our resolve to preserve world peace and freedom. That this nation will once again be strong enough to to that.

In his Inaugural Address, President Reagan repeated his determination and spoke again of the national commitment to peace and to the necessary strength to secure that peace.

As for enemies of freedom, those who are potential adversaries, they will be reminded that peace is the highest aspiration of the American people. We will negotiate for it, sacrifice for it; we will not surrender for it—now or ever.

Our forebearance should never be misunderstood. Our reluctance for conflict should not be misjudged as a failure of will.

When action is required to preserve our national security, we will act. We will maintain sufficient strength to prevail if need be, knowing that if we do, we have the best chance of never having to use that strength.

Above all, we must realize that no arsenal or no weapon in the arsenals of the world is so formidable as the will and moral courage of free men and women.

It is a weapon that our adversaries in today's world do not have.

It is a weapon that we as Americans do have.

Let that be understood by those who practice terrorism and prey upon their neighbors.

Just days after his Inauguration, President Reagan welcomed home the U.S. hostages who had been held captive in Iran. He served notice to the world that it was not his intention to allow a similar fate to ever befall Americans again.

Those henceforth in the representation of this nation will be accorded every means of protection that America can offer. Let terrorists beware that when the rules of international behavior are violated, our policy will be one of swift and effective retribution.

We hear it said that we live in a time when there are limits to our powers. Well, let is also be understood, there are limits to our patience.

During his first year in office, President Reagan also delivered the commencement address at the United States Military Academy. He told those young men and women about to enter the service of their country of his appreciation for their dedication and their patriotism and assured them they had the backing of the entire nation.

I accept without question the words of George Washington: "To be prepared for war is one of the most effectual means of preserving the peace."

A truly successful army is one that, because of its strength and ability and dedication, will not be called upon to fight because no one will dare to provoke it.

There have been four wars in my lifetime; none of them came about because the United States was too strong. At the end of World War II, we alone were at the peak of our military strength, our great industrial capacity was untouched by war's destruction, and it was then that—in those dark days—that Pope Pius XII said, "America has a great genius for great and unselfish deeds. Into the hands of America God has placed an afflicted mankind."

Let friend and foe alike be made aware of the spirit that is sweeping across our land, because it means we will meet our responsibilities to the free world. Very much a part of this new spirit is patriotism, and with that goes a heartfelt appreciation for the sacrifices of those in uniform.

In his 1982 State of the Union Address, his first, President Reagan reminded Congress that America's strength is essential, not only for our own defense but that of our allies as well.

Our foreign policy is a policy of strength, fairness and balance. By restoring America's military credibility, by pursuing peace at the negotiating table wherever both sides are willing to sit down in good faith, and by regaining the respect of America's allies and adversaries alike, we have strengthened our country's position as a force for peace and progress in the world.

Building a more peaceful world requires a sound strategy and the national resolve to back it up. When radical forces threaten our friends, when economic misfortune creates conditions of instability, when strategically vital parts of the world fall under the shadow of Soviet power, our response can make the difference between peaceful change or disorder and violence. That's why we've laid such stress not only on our own defense, but on our vital foreign assistance program. Your recent passage of the foreign assistance act sent a signal to the world that America will not shrink from making the investments necessary for both peace and security. Our foreign policy must be rooted in realism, not naiveté or self-delusion.

On Memorial Day, 1982, addressing a gathering at Arlington National Cemetery, President Reagan reminded the nation that we owe it to the memory of all those who have gone before us, who have given their lives for us, to protect and preserve the precious gift for which they fought.

War will not come again, other young men will not have to die, if we will speak honestly of the dangers that confront us and remain strong enough to meet those dangers.

Our goal is peace. We can gain that peace by strengthening our alliances, by speaking candidly of the dangers before us, by assuring potential adversaries of our seriousness, by actively pursuing every chance of honest and fruitful negotiation.

The willingness of some to give their lives so that others might live never fails to evoke in us a sense of wonder and mystery.

And how they must have wished, in all the ugliness that war brings, that no other generation of young men to follow would have to undergo that same experience.

As we honor their memory today, let us pledge that their lives, their sacrifices, their valor shall be justified and remembered for as long as God gives life to this nation.

And let us also pledge to do our utmost to carry out what must have been their wish: that no other generation of young men will ever have to share their experience and repeat their sacrifice.

Earlier today, with the music that we have heard and that of our national anthem—I can't claim to know the words of all the national anthems in the world, but I don't know of any other that ends with a question and a challenge as ours does:

Does that flag still wave o'er the land of the free and the home of the brave?

That is what we must resolve.

In his address to the British Parliament June 8, 1982, he repeated the need to maintain a strong military while clinging firmly to the hope that it would never have to be tested.

Our military strength is a prerequisite to peace, but let

it be clear that we maintain this strength in the hope it
will never be used. For the ultimate determinant in the
struggle now going on for the world will not be bombs or
rockets, but a test of wills and ideas—a trial of spiritual
resolve: the values we hold, the beliefs we cherish, the
ideals to which we are dedicated.

*And the next day he reconfirmed to the West German
Parliament the commitment of the United States to our
allies and friends.*

Our adversaries would be foolishly mistaken should
they gamble that Americans would abandon their alliance
responsibilities, no matter how severe the test.

*On November 22, 1982, President Reagan addressed the
American people on the subject of arms control, including
a discussion of the MX missile. He told us that he shared
the desire of many to see a reduction in armaments, particularly nuclear weapons, but that such goals were unrealistic
without a change in circumstances.*

This nation's military objective has always been to
maintain peace by preventing war.

And yes, it is sadly ironic that in these modern times, it
still takes weapons to prevent war. I wish it did not.

You often hear that the United States and the Soviet
Union are in an arms race. Well, the truth is that the
Soviet Union has raced, we have not.

The United States wants deep cuts in the world's arsenal of weapons, but unless we demonstrate the will to
rebuild our strength and restore the military balance, the
Soviets, since they are so far ahead, have little incentive
to negotiate with us. Let me repeat that point because it
goes to the heart of our policies. Unless we demonstrate
the will to rebuild our strength, the Soviets will have little
incentive to negotiate.

If we had not begun to modernize, the Soviet negotiators
would know that we had nothing to bargain with except
talk. They would know that we were bluffing without a
good hand because they know what cards we hold just as
we know what is in their hand.

In his March 23, 1983 speech to the American people on "Peace and National Security," the President set forth an analytical approach to the matter of providing for a safe, secure America, how we came to be so threatened, and what we need to do to overcome that threat.

The defense of the United States is based on a simple premise: The United States does not start fights. We will never be an aggressor. We maintain our strength in order to deter and defend against aggression—to preserve freedom and peace.

Since the dawn of the atomic age, we have sought to reduce the risk of war by maintaining a strong deterrent and by seeking genuine arms control. Deterrence means simply this: Making sure any adversary who thinks about attacking the United States or our allies or our vital interests concludes that the risks to him outweigh any potential gains. Once he understands that, he won't attack. We maintain the peace through our strength; weakness only invites aggression.

It took one kind of military force to deter an attack when we had far more nuclear weapons than any other power; it takes another kind now that the Soviets, for example, have enough accurate and powerful weapons to destroy virtually all of our missiles on the ground.

As the Soviets have increased their military power, they have been emboldened to extend that power. They are spreading their military influence in ways that can directly challenge our vital interests and those of our allies.

Every item in our defense program—our ships, our tanks, our planes, our funds for training and spare parts— is intended for one all-important purpose—to keep the peace.

I know that all of you want peace and so do I. I know too that many of you seriously believe that a nuclear freeze would further the cause of peace. But a freeze now would make us less, not more, secure and would raise, not reduce, the risks of war. It would be largely unverifiable and would seriously undercut our negotiations on arms reduction. It would reward the Soviets for their massive military build-up while preventing us from modernizing our aging and increasingly vulnerable forces. With their present margin of superiority, why should they agree to arms reductions knowing that we were prohibited from catching up?

One of the tragic ironies of history—and we've seen it happen more than once in this century—is the way that tyrannical systems, whose military strength is based on oppressing their people, grow strong while, through wishful thinking, free societies allow themselves to be lulled into a false sense of security.

It is up to us, in our time, to choose, and choose wisely, between the hard but necessary task of preserving peace and freedom and the temptation to ignore our duty and blindly hope for the best while the enemies of freedom grow stronger day by day.

Eight days later, in his address to the Los Angeles World Affairs Council, President Reagan expanded on his earlier discussion of the nuclear freeze movement and why the concept is not a wise choice for America today.

This is our dilemma, and it is a powerful one: We must both defend freedom and preserve the peace. We must stand true to our principles and our friends while preventing a holocaust.

Coming into office, I made two promises to the American people about peace and security: I promised them to restore our neglected defenses in order to strengthen and preserve peace, and I promised to pursue reliable agreements to reduce nuclear weapons. Both these promises are being kept.

The freeze concept is dangerous for many reasons:

—It would preserve today's high, unequal and unstable levels of nuclear forces, and by so doing, reduce Soviet incentives to negotiate for real reductions.

—It would pull the rug out from under our negotiators in Geneva, as they have testified. After all, why should the Soviets negotiate if they have already achieved a freeze in a position of advantage to them?

—Also, some think a freeze would be easy to agree on, but it raises enormously complicated problems of what is to be frozen, how it is to be achieved and, most of all, verified. Attempting to negotiate these critical details would only divert us from the goal of negotiating reductions, for who knows how long.

—The freeze proposal would also make a lot more sense if a similar movement against nuclear weapons were putting similar pressures on Soviet leaders in Moscow. As former Secretary of Defense Harold Brown has pointed out, the effect of the freeze "is to put pressure on the United States, but not the Soviet Union."

—Finally, the freeze would reward the Soviets for their 15-year buildup while locking us into our existing equipment, which in many cases is obsolete and badly in need of modernization. Three-quarters of Soviet strategic warheads are on delivery systems five years old or less; three-quarters of the American strategic warheads are on delivery systems 15 years old or older. The time comes when everything wears out—the trouble is, it comes a lot sooner for us than for them. And, under a freeze, we couldn't do anything about it."

On October 27, 1983, President Reagan addressed the American people on the dual subjects of the bombing of U.S. marine headquarters in Beirut, Lebanon, and the rescue mission that sent American military forces into the island of Grenada to bring out the approximately 1,000 Americans confined there under the terms of a "shoot-to-kill curfew."

Supporters and critics alike called it one of his best speeches ever as President of the United States. In agreement with that opinion, several passages have been selected for inclusion.

In the year that our marines have been there, Lebanon has made important steps toward stability and order. The physical presence of the marines lends support to both the Lebanese Government and its army. It allows the hard work of diplomacy to go forward. Indeed, without the peacekeepers from the U.S., France, Italy and Britain, the efforts to find a peaceful solution in Lebanon would collapse.

We have strong circumstantial evidence that the attack on our marines was directed by terrorists who used the same method to destroy our embassy in Beirut. Those who directed this atrocity must be dealt justice, and they will be.

Beyond our progress in Lebanon, let us remember that our main goal and purpose is to achieve a broader peace in all of the Middle East. The functions and bitterness that we see in Lebanon are just a microcosm of the difficulties that are spread across much of that region. A peace initiative for the entire Middle East, consistent with the Camp David accord, and U.N. Resolutions 242 and 338, still offers the best hope for bringing peace to the region.

Let me ask those who say we should get out of Lebanon: If we were to leave Lebanon now, what message would that send to those who foment instability and terrorism? If America were to walk away from Lebanon, what chance would there be for a negotiated settlement producing the unified, democratic Lebanon? If we turned our backs on Lebanon now, what would be the future of Israel?

Can the United States, or the free world, for that matter, stand by and see the Middle East incorporated into the Soviet bloc?

Brave young men have been taken from us. Many others have been grievously wounded. Are we to tell them their sacrifice was wasted, when they gave their lives in defense of our national security as much as any man who ever died fighting in a war?

We must not strip every ounce of meaning and purpose from their courageous sacrifice. We are a nation with global responsibilities. We're not somewhere else in the world protecting someone else's interest. We're there protecting our own.

It should be noted that in all the planning, a top priority was to minimize risk, to avoid casualties to our own men and also the Grenadian forces as much as humanly possible. But there were casualties. And we all owe a debt to those who lost their lives or were wounded. They were few in number but even one is a tragic price to pay.

It's our intention to get our men out as soon as possible.

The events in Lebanon and Grenada, though oceans apart, are closely related. Not only has Moscow assisted and encouraged the violence in both countries, but it provides direct support through a network of surrogates and terrorists. It is no coincidence that when the thugs tried to wrest control of Grenada, there were 30 Soviet advisers and hundreds of Cuban military and paramilitary forces on the island.

Now there was a time when our national security was based on a standing army here within our own borders and shore batteries of artillery along our coast, and of course a navy to keep the sea lanes open for the shipping of things necessary to our well being. The world has changed. Today our national security can be threatened in far-away places. It's up to all of us to be aware of the strategic importance of such places and to be able to identify them.

Sam Rayburn once said that freedom is not something a nation can work for once and win forever. He said it's like an insurance policy, its premiums must be kept up to date. In order to keep it, we have to keep working for it and sacrificing for it just as long as we live. If we do not, our children may not know the pleasure of working to keep it for it may not be theirs to keep.

That marine, and all others like him living and dead, have been faithful to their ideals. They've given willingly of themselves so that a nearly defenseless people in a region of great strategic importance to the free world will have a chance someday to live lives free of murder and mayhem and terrorism. I think that young marine and all of his comrades have given every one of us something to live up to.

They were not afraid to stand up for their country or no matter how difficult and slow the journey might be, to give to others that last best hope of a better future.

We cannot and will not dishonor them now and the sacrifices they made by failing to remain as faithful to the cause of freedom and the pursuit of peace as they have been.

CHAPTER 5

Our only purpose—
one all people share—
is to search for ways to reduce
the danger of nuclear war.

While working to strengthen America's military as a deterrent to war, President Reagan has been working just as diligently to secure a true reduction in nuclear arms. This, too, however, has been approached with the same realism that has led the President to strengthen our military in the first place.

During the 1980 presidential campaign, he discussed his approach to arms limitation agreements during an interview with the Associated Press.

My objection to Salt II is not arms limitation. It legitimizes the arms race. It begins by letting the Soviet Union build 3,000 more warheads, then we can build some to catch up, only we can't catch up until 1990. I think it is a fatally flawed treaty, and it isn't arms limitation. If we're really going to try to remove the danger to the world today, let's sit down with the intention voiced and the agreement of the other side that we're going to find a way to fairly reduce the strategic weapons (of both sides) so that neither of us can threaten the other.

I don't think we should sit at the table the same way we have in the past. We have been unilaterally disarming at the same time we're negotiating supposed arms limitations with the other fellow, where all he has to do is sit there and not give up anything and his superiority increases. He will be far more inclined to negotiate in good faith if he knows that the United States is engaged in building up its military. They know our industrial strength. They know our capacity. The one card that's been missing in these negotiations has been the possibility of an arms race. Now the Soviets have been racing, but with no competition. No one else is racing. And so I think we'd get a lot farther at the table if they know that as they continue, they're faced with our industrial capacity and all that we can do.

In November, 1981, President Reagan addressed the National Press Club in Washington. Referring to his stay in the hospital after the assassination attempt, he told of having a lot of time for reflection. He told his audience the story of a letter he composed and sent to Soviet President Brezhnev while in the hospital and then later announced the moves he was taking to help secure a reduction in the threat to mankind posed by nuclear weapons.

Of his hospital stay, he said:

One day I decided to send a personal, hand-written letter to Soviet President Leonid Brezhnev, reminding him that we had met about 10 years ago in San Clemente, California, as he and President Nixon were concluding a series of meetings that had brought hope to all the world. Never had peace and good will seemed closer at hand.

I'd like to read you a few paragraphs from that letter:

"Mr. President, when we met I asked if you were aware that the hopes and aspirations of millions of people throughout the world were dependent on the decisions that would be reached in those meetings. You took my hand in both of yours and assured me that you were aware of that and that you were dedicated with all your heart and soul and mind to fulfilling those hopes and dreams."

I went on in my letter to say: "The people of the world still share that hope. Indeed, the peoples of the world, despite differences in racial and ethnic origin, have very much in common. They want the dignity of having some control over their individual lives, their destiny. They want to work at the trade or craft of their own choosing and to be fairly rewarded.

"They want to raise their families in peace, without harming anyone or suffering harm themselves. Government exists for their convenience, not the other way around. If they're incapable, as some would have us believe, of self-government, then where among them do we find any who are capable of governing others? Is it possible that we have permitted ideology, political and economic philosophies and governmental policies to keep us from considering the very real everyday problems of our peoples?

"Will the average Soviet family be better off, or even aware, that the Soviet Union has imposed a government of its own choice on the people of Afghanistan? Is life better for the people of Cuba because the Cuban military dictates who shall govern the people of Angola? It is often implied that such things have been made necessary because of territorial ambitions of the United States; that we have imperialistic designs and they thus constitute a threat to your own security and that of the newly emerging nations.

"There is not only no evidence to support such a charge, there is solid evidence that the United States, when it could have dominated the world with no risk to itself, made no effort whatsoever to do so. When World War II ended, the United States had the only undamaged industrial power in the world. Our military might was at its peak, and we alone had the ultimate weapon—the nuclear —weapon with the unquestioned ability to deliver it anywhere in the world. If we had sought world domination then, who would have opposed us?

"But the United States followed a different course, one unique in all the history of mankind. We used our power and wealth to rebuild the war-ravaged economies of the world, including those of the nations who had been our enemies. May I say there is absolutely no substance to charges that the United States is guilty of imperialism or attempts to impose its will on other countries by use of force."

I concluded my letter by saying, "Mr. President, should we not be concerned with eliminating the obstacles which prevent our people—those you and I represent—from achieving their most cherished goals?"

Later in the National Press Club, President Reagan outlined his concrete proposals for nuclear arms reductions.

As part of the 1979 two-track decision, NATO made a commitment to seek arms control negotiations with the Soviet Union on intermediate-range nuclear forces. The United States has been preparing for these negotiations through close consultation with our NATO partners. We're now ready to set forth our proposal.

I have informed President Brezhnev that when our delegation travels to the negotiations on intermediate-range land-based nuclear missiles in Geneva on the 30th of this month, my representatives will present the following proposal:

The United States is prepared to cancel its deployment of Pershing 2 and ground-launched missiles if the Soviets will dismantle their SS-20, SS-4 and SS-5 missiles. This would be an historic step.

With Soviet agreement, we could together substantially reduce the dread threat of nuclear war which hangs over the people of Europe. This, like the first footstep on the moon, would be a giant step for mankind.

Today I've announced an agenda that can help to achieve peace, security and freedom across the globe. In particular, I have made an important offer to forgo entirely deployment of new American missiles in Europe if the Soviet Union is prepared to respond on an equal footing.

There is no reason why people in any part of the world should have to live in permanent fear of war or its specter. I believe the time has come for all nations to act in a responsible spirit that doesn't threaten other states. I believe the time is right to move forward on arms control and the resolution of critical regional disputes at the conference table. Nothing will have a higher priority for me and for the American people over the coming months and years.

Addressing the United Nations 20 years ago, another American president described the goal that we still pursue today. He said, "If we can all persevere, if we can look beyond our shores and ambitions, then surely the age will dawn in which the strong are just and the weak secure and the peace preserved." He didn't live to see that goal achieved.

I invite all nations to join with America today in the quest for such a world.

President Reagan also told the students graduating from Eureka College in May 1982, of his commitment to reduce the threat of nuclear war by reducing nuclear weapons, fairly and equitably.

The monumental task of reducing and reshaping our strategic forces to enhance stability will take many years of concentrated effort. But I believe that it will be possible to reduce the risks of war by removing the instabilities that now exist and by removing the nuclear menace.

I will tell President Brezhnev that the United States is ready to build a new understanding based upon the principles I have outlined here today. I will tell him that his Government and his people have nothing to fear from the United States. The free nations living at peace in the world community can vouch for the fact that we seek only harmony. And I will ask President Brezhnev why our two nations cannot practice mutual restraint. Why can't our peoples enjoy the benefits that would flow from real cooperation? Why can't we reduce the number of horrendous weapons?

Perhaps I should also speak to him of this school and the young graduates who are leaving it today—of your hopes for the future, of your deep desire for peace, and yet your strong commitment to defend your values if threatened. Perhaps if he could someday attend such a ceremony as this, he would better understand America. In the only system he knows, you would be here by the decision of government and on this day the government would be represented here telling many of you where you were going to work after your graduation.

And he told the delegates gathered at the United Nations for the Disarmament Session that reducing the threat of war is a debt that every world leader owes to the people he or she represents.

What a better world it would be if the guns were silenced, if neighbor no longer encroached on neighbor and all peoples were free to reap the rewards of their toil and determine their own destiny and system of government whatever their choice.

As both patriots of our nations and the hope of all the world let those of us assembled here in the name of peace deepen our understandings, renew our commitment to the rule of law and take new and bolder steps to calm an uneasy world.

Can any delegate here deny that in so doing he would be doing what the people, the rank and file of his own country or her own country want him or her to do. Isn't it time for us to really represent the deepest, most heartfelt yearnings of all of our people.

Let no nation abuse this common longing to be free of fear. We must not manipulate our people by playing upon their nightmares. We must serve mankind through genuine disarmament.

With God's help, we can secure life and freedom for generations to come.

In his 1983 State of the Union message, President Reagan spoke to the Congress of the need to maintain strength so that we could make real moves toward reductions.

But our strategy for peace with freedom must also be based on strength—economic and military strength. A strong American economy is essential to the well-being and security of our friends and allies.

Deep down, the Soviets must know it is in their interest as well as ours to prevent a wasteful arms race. And once they recognize our unshakeable resolve to maintain adequate deterrence, they will have every reason to join us in the search for greater security and major arms reduction. When that moment comes—and I am confident that it will—we will have taken an important step toward a more peaceful future for all the world's people.

But it was on March 23, 1983, in what some people have called his most daring and courageous speech ever, that President Reagan made perhaps the most significant proposal to remove the threat of nuclear holocaust by implementation of a spaceborne, non-nuclear defense system. It has often been compared to President John F. Kennedy's commitment to put an American on the moon "within the decade."

My predecessors in the Oval Office have appeared before you on other occasions to describe the threat posed by Soviet power and have proposed steps to address that threat. But since the advent of nuclear weapons, those steps have been directed toward deterrence of aggression through the promise of retaliation—the notion that no rational nation would launch an attack that would inevitably result in unacceptable losses to themselves. This approach to stability has worked. We and our allies have succeeded in preventing nuclear war for three decades. In recent months, however, my advisors, including the Joint Chiefs of Staff, have underscored the bleakness of the future before us.

Over the course of these discussions, I have become more and more deeply convinced that the human spirit must be capable of rising above dealing with other nations and human beings by threatening their existence. Feeling this way, I believe we must thoroughly examine every opportunity for reducing tensions and for introducing greater stability into the strategic calculus on both sides. One of the most important contributions we can make is, of course, to lower the level of all arms, and particularly nuclear arms. We are engaged right now in several negotiations with the Soviet Union to bring about a mutual reduction of weapons. I will report to you a week from tomorrow my thoughts on that score. But let me just say I am totally committed to this course.

If the Soviet Union will join with us in our effort to achieve major arms reduction we will have succeeded in stabilizing the nuclear balance. Nevertheless, it will still be necessary to rely on the specter of retaliation—on mutual threat, and that is a sad commentary on the human condition.

Would it not be better to save lives than to avenge them? Are we not capable of demonstrating our peaceful intentions by applying all our abilities and our ingenuity to achieving a truly lasting stability? I think we are—indeed, we must!

After careful consultation with my advisors, including the Joint Chiefs of Staff, I believe there is a way. Let me share with you a vision of the future which offers hope. It is that we embark on a program to counter the awesome Soviet missile threat with measures that are defensive. Let us turn to the very strengths in technology that spawned our great industrial base and that have given us the quality of life we enjoy today.

Up until now we have increasingly based our strategy of deterrence upon the threat of retaliation. But what if free people could live secure in the knowledge that their security did not rest upon the threat of instant U.S. retaliation to deter a Soviet attack; that we could intercept and destroy strategic ballistic missiles before they reached our own soil or that of our allies?

I know this is a formidable task, one that may not be accomplished before the end of this century. Yet, current technology has attained a level of sophistication where it is reasonable for us to begin this effort. It will take years, probably decades, of effort on many fronts. There will be failures and setbacks, just as there will be successes and breakthroughs. And as we proceed we must remain constant in preserving the nuclear deterrent and maintaining a solid capability for flexible response. But is it not worth every investment necessary to free the world from the threat of nuclear war? We know it is!

In the meantime, we will continue to pursue real reductions in nuclear arms, negotiating from a position of strength that can be insured only by modernizing our strategic forces. At the same time, we must take steps to reduce the risk of a conventional military conflict escalating into nuclear war by improving our nonnuclear capabilities. America does possess—now—the technologies to attain very significant improvements in the effectiveness of our conventional, nonnuclear forces. Proceeding boldly with these new technologies, we can significantly reduce any incentive that the Soviet Union may have to threaten attack against the United States or its allies.

As we pursue our goal of defensive technologies, we recognize that our allies rely upon our strategic offensive power to deter attacks against them. Their vital interests and ours are inextricably linked—their safety and ours are one. And no change in technology can or will alter that reality. We must and shall continue to honor our commitments.

I clearly recognize that defensive systems have limitations and raise certain problems and ambiguities. If paired with offensive systems, they can be viewed as fostering an aggressive policy and no one wants that.

But with these considerations firmly in mind, I call upon the scientific community who gave us nuclear weapons to turn their great talents to the cause of mankind and world peace; to give us the means of rendering these nuclear weapons impotent and obsolete.

Tonight, consistent with our obligations under the ABM

Treaty and recognizing the need for close consultation with our allies, I am taking an important first step. I am directing a comprehensive and intensive program to begin to achieve our ultimate goal of eliminating the threat posed by strategic nuclear missiles. This could pave the way for arms control measures to eliminate the weapons themselves. We seek neither military superiority nor political advantage. Our only purpose—one all people share—is to search for ways to reduce the danger of nuclear war.

My fellow Americans, tonight we are launching an effort which holds the purpose of changing the course of human history. There will be risks and results take time. But with your support, I believe we can do it.

CHAPTER 6

"... Government is not the solution to our
problem: Government is the problem."

*Throughout his political career, Ronald Reagan has
been a stalwart proponent of fiscal conservatism. He believes firmly in the need for a sound, strong economy—one
that avoids runaway inflation and provides the opportunity for the American free enterprise system to function in
the manner in which it was created and developed.*

*And, at the same time, he has always maintained that
the only way our economy can ever get out of control is when
we let our government get out of control.*

*There was a temptation in this section to divide it into
two sections, one dealing with the needs and methods for
a strong economy and the other on the necessity of bringing
government back under the control of-the people. The two
are so inextricably entwined, however, that such a division
proved infeasible.*

*In "A Time for Choosing," near the end of the 1964 presi-
dential campaign, Ronald Reagan reminded his audience
of what we had allowed to happen to our government.*

Since the beginning of the century, our gross national
product has increased by 33 times. In the same period, the
cost of federal government has increased 234 times and
while the work force is only one and a half times greater,
federal employees number nine times as many.

*In his inaugural address as Governor of California, Gov-
ernor Reagan told of the need to bring government under
control, and of his unwillingness to accept the notion that
it couldn't be done.*

For many years now, you and I have been shushed like
children and told there are no simple answers to the complex questions which are beyond our comprehension. Well,
the truth is, there are simple answers—there just are not

easy ones. The time has come for us to decide whether collectively we can afford everything and anything we think of simply because we think of it. The time has come to run a check to see if all the services government provides were in answer to demands or were just goodies dreamed up for our supposed betterment. The time has come to match outgo to income, instead of always doing it the other way around.

But, as also will become apparent throughout this section and elsewhere in this book, it was never Ronald Reagan's intention to reduce government spending by ending assistance programs for those truly in need.

With that in mind, it's interesting to note here that Ronald Reagan was once asked to look back on his eight years as Governor of California and list what he felt were his most important accomplishments.

The two things I'm most proud of in those years were, first, the restoration of solvency to the state, getting it out of debt and then returning to the taxpayers some 5.7 billion dollars in tax rebates; and second, the welfare reforms which reduced the rolls by some three hundred thousand people who were not really eligible for help. We saved the taxpayers two billion dollars in three years and raised the grants to the deserving needy by forty three percent.

In 1968, Governor Reagan addressed the Economic Club of New York and spoke of the concern of the American people about their federal government.

At the moment, there appears to be a panic fear afloat in the air, partly due to a feeling of helplessness, a feeling that government is now a separate force beyond their control, that their voices echo unheeded in the vast and multitudinous halls of government. I do not remember a time when so many Americans, regardless of their economic or social standing, have been so suspicious and apprehensive of the aims, the credibility, and the competence of the federal establishment. There is a question abroad in the land: "What is happening to us?"

Five years later, the federal government was in even greater turmoil. The day after President Richard Nixon resigned, Ronald Reagan addressed the National Young

*Republicans at Lake Tahoe. Part of his message of reassur-
ance was that the Republican party and the conservative
movement in America were both sound and would play an
important role in restoring health to our nation.*

You can have faith in the Republican philosophy of
fiscal common sense, limited government and individual
freedom.

Government alone is the cause of inflation.

No government is ever justified in spending a single
dollar more than necessary for legitimate functions. And
no government should ever tolerate abuses, legal or ille-
gal, that not only defraud the people government is trying
to help, but increase the taxes of those working citizens
who finance our efforts to help the poor, the aged and the
infirm.

*In his January 1977 speech before the Intercollegiate
Studies Institute, discussing the new conservative movement in America, Ronald Reagan spoke of the change in
the attitude of the American people toward their government.*

Little more than a decade ago, more than two-thirds of
Americans believed the federal Government could solve
all our problems with its multitude of bureaus, agencies,
and programs, without restricting our freedom or bank-
rupting the nation.

We warned of things to come; of the danger inherent in
unwarranted government involvement in things not in its
proper province. And today, more than two thirds of our
citizens are telling us, and each other, that social engineer-
ing by the federal Government has failed. The Great Society is great only in power, in size, and in cost. Freedom has
been diminished and we stand on the brink of economic
ruin.

*Later that same year, in September, Ronald Reagan ad-
dressed the Executive Club of Chicago. His message—"Let
the People Rule."*

The ills of a nation stem from a single source: the belief
that government, particularly the federal government,
has the answer to our ills and that the proper method of
dealing with social problems is to transfer power from the

private sector to the public sector and within the public sector, from state and local governments to the ultimate power center in Washington.

By taxing and consuming an ever greater share of the national wealth, it has imposed an intolerable burden of taxation on American citizens. By spending above and beyond even this level of inflation, it has created the horrendous inflation of the past decade. And by saddling our economy with an ever-greater burden of controls and regulations, it has generated economic problems—from the raising of consumer prices to the destruction of jobs, to choking off vital supplies of energy.

When he accepted his party's nomination as their presidential candidate, Ronald Reagan told those assembled in Detroit that tackling the runaway economy, and runaway government, would be among his primary concerns.

My view of government places trust not in one person or one party, but in those values that transcend persons and parties. The trust is where it belongs—in the people. The responsibility to live up to that trust is where it belongs, in their elected leaders. That kind of relationship, between the people and their elected leaders, is a special kind of compact.

As your nominee, I pledge to you to restore to the Federal Government the capacity to do the people's work without dominating their lives. I pledge to you a Government that will not only work well but wisely, its ability to act tempered by prudence, and its willingness to do good balanced by the knowledge that government is never more dangerous than when our desire to have it help us blinds us to its great power to harm us.

High taxes, we are told, are somehow good for us, as if, when government spends our money it isn't inflationary, but when we spend it, it is.

We must have the clarity of vision to see the difference between what is essential and what is merely desirable; and then the courage to bring our Government back under control.

It is essential that we maintain both the forward

momentum of economic growth and the strength of the safety net between those in our society who need our help. We also believe it is essential that the integrity of all aspects of Social Security be preserved.

I believe it is clear our Federal Government is overgrown and overweight. Indeed, it is time our Government should go on a diet.

We are going to put an end to the money merry-go-round where our money becomes Washington's money, to be spent by states and cities exactly the way the Federal bureaucracies tell us it has to be spent.

I will not accept the excuse that the Federal Government has grown so big and powerful that it is beyond the control of any President, any Administration or Congress. We are going to put an end to the notion that the American taxpayer exists to fund the Federal Government. The Federal Government exists to serve the American people.

Given the state of the American economy, it came as no surprise that economic considerations arose frequently during the 1980 presidential campaign. In a televised debate with President Carter during that campaign, Ronald Reagan was asked how he would go about reducing government spending.

Well, most people when they think about cutting government spending, they think in terms of eliminating unnecessary programs or wiping out something, some service that government is supposed to perform. I believe there is enough extravagance and fat in government. As a matter of fact, one of the secretaries of Health Education and Welfare under Mr. Carter testified that he thought there was $7 billion worth of fraud and waste in welfare, and in the medical programs associated with it. We've had the General Accounting Office estimate that there are probably tens of billions of dollars lost on fraud alone, and they have added that waste adds even more to that.

In a campaign speech before the International Busines Council in Chicago, Ronald Reagan dealt with how government interference in business, in the free enterprise system, was worsening our economic situation on almost a daily basis.

We must move boldly, decisively, and quickly to control the runaway growth of Federal spending, to remove the tax disincentives that are throttling the economy, and to reform the regulatory web that is smothering it.

We must have, and I am proposing, a new strategy for the 1980's.

Only a series of well-planned economic actions, taken so that they complement and reinforce one another, can move our economy forward again.

We must keep the level of government spending at reasonable and prudent levels.

We must reduce personal income tax rates and accelerate and simplify depreciation schedules in an orderly, systematic way to remove disincentives to work, savings, investment and productivity.

We must review regulations that affect the economy and change them to encourage economic growth.

We must establish a stable, sound and predictable monetary policy.

And we must restore confidence by following a consistent national economic policy that does not change from month to month.

Government regulation, like fire, makes a good servant but a bad master.

No one can argue with the intent of this regulation—to improve health and safety and to give us cleaner air and water—but too often regulations work against rather than for the interests of the people. When the real take home pay of the American worker is declining steadily, and 8 million Americans are out of work, we must carefully reexamine our regulatory structure to assess to what degree regulations have contributed to this situation. In my administration there should and will be a thorough and systematic review of the thousands of federal regulations that affect the economy.

Let's get America working again.
The time is now.

As the day of election drew near, Ronald Reagan delivered some of his most eloquent speeches ever on our national economy and our federal government.

Many Americans today, just as they did 200 years ago, feel burdened, stifled and sometimes even oppressed by government that has grown too large, too bureaucratic, too wasteful, too unresponsive, too uncaring about people and their problems. I believe we can embark on a new age of reform in this country and an era of national renewal, an era that will reorder the relationship between citizen and government, that will make government again responsive to the people, that will revitalize the values of family, work and neighborhood and that will restore our private and independent social institutions. These institutions always have served as both buffer and bridge between the individual and the state—and these institutions, not government, are the real sources of our economic growth and progress as a people.

That's why I've said throughout this campaign that we must control and limit the growth of federal spending, that we must reduce tax rates to stimulate work and savings and investment. That's why I've said we can relieve labor and business of burdensome, unecessary regulations and still maintain high standards of environmental and occupational safety.

That's why I've said we can reduce the cost of government by eliminating billions lost to waste and fraud in the Federal bureaucracy—a problem that is now an unrelenting national scandal. And because we're a federation of sovereign states, we can restore the health and vitality of state and local governments by returning to them control over programs best run at those levels of government closer to the people. We can fight corruption while we work to bring into our government men and women of competence and high integrity.

The speech Ronald Reagan made to the American people on the eve of the 1980 election, which he called "A Vision for America," was one of the most moving I have ever witnessed. There were some news reports that tears came to my eyes as I watched it being taped in Peoria. I will not deny that account.

Who could forget these words, however, thrown out in challenge to the American people:

Consider these questions as well when you make your final decision:

Are you more confident that our economy will create productive work for our society or are you less confident?

Are you satisfied that inflation at the highest rates in thirty-three years were the best we could do? Are interest rates at 14½ percent something you are prepared to live with?

Are you pleased with the ability of young people to buy a home; or the elderly to live their remaining lives in happiness; of our youngsters to take pride in the world we have built for them?

Is our nation stronger and more capable of leading the world toward peace and freedom or is it weaker?

Is there more stability in the world or less?

Are you convinced that we have earned the respect of the world and our allies, or has America's position across the globe diminished?

Are you personally more secure in your life? Is your family more secure? Is America safer in the world?

And most importantly—quite simply—the basic question of our lives: Are you happier today than when Mr. Carter became President of the United States?

In his Inaugural Address, President Reagan set the tone for his administration and its approach to solving America's economic difficulties.

In this present crisis, government is not the solution to our problem; government is the problem.

We are a nation that has a government—not the other way around. And this makes us special among the nations of the earth.

Our Government has no power except that granted it by the people. It is time to check and reverse the growth of government which shows signs of having grown beyond the consent of the governed.

Now, so there will be no misunderstanding, it's not my intention to do away with government.

It is rather to make it work—work with us, not over us; to stand by our side, not ride on our back. Government can and must provide opportunity, not smother it; foster productivity, not stifle it.

It is no coincidence that our present troubles parallel and are porportionate to the intervention and intrusion in our lives that result from unnecessary and excessive growth of Government.

Almost immediately after he took office, on February 5, 1981, President Reagan went on national television to address the American public on the true state of affairs, or as the speech was called, "The State of the Nation's Economy."

He spoke in detail of how we had lost our position of industrial leadership in the world and, more importantly, he addressed the reasons why it happened and what we needed to do to overcome that loss.

Today this once great industrial giant of ours has the lowest rate of gain in productivity in virtually all the industrial nations with whom we must compete in the world market. We can't even hold our own market here in America against foreign automobiles, steel and a number of other products.

Japanese production of automobiles is almost twice as great per worker as it is in America.

Japanese steelworkers out-produce their American counterparts by about 25 percent.

This isn't because they are better workers. I'll match the American working man or woman against anyone in the world. But we have to give them the modern tools and equipment that workers in the other industrial nations have.

We invented the assembly line and mass production, but punitive tax policies and excessive and unnecessary regulations plus Government borrowing have stifled our ability to update plant and equipment. When capital investment is made, it is too often for some unproductive alterations demanded by Government to meet various of its regulations.

Excessive taxation of individuals has robbed us of incentive and made overtime unprofitable.

We once produced about 40 percent of the world's steel. We now produce 19 percent.

We were once the greatest producer of automobiles, producing more than all the rest of the world combined. That is no longer true, and in addition, the big three, the major automobile companies in our land, have sustained tremendous losses in the past year and have been forced to lay off thousands of workers.

All of you who are working know that even with cost of living pay raises, you can't keep up with inflation. In our progressive tax system, as you increase the number of dollars you earn, you find yourself moved up into higher tax brackets, paying a higher tax rate just for trying to hold your own. The result? Your standard of living is going down.

Over the past decades, we've talked of curtailing Government spending so that we can then lower the tax burden. Sometimes we've even taken a run at doing that. But there were always those who told us that taxes couldn't be cut until spending was reduced. Well, we can lecture our children about extravagance until we run out of voice and breath. Or we can cure their extravagance simply by reducing their allowance.

It is time to recognize that we have come to a turning point. We are threatened with an economic calamity of tremendous proportions and the old business as usual treatment can't save us.

Together we must chart a different course. We must increase productivity. That means making it possible for industry to modernize and make use of the technology which we ourselves invented; and that means above all bringing Government spending back within Government revenues which is the only way, together with increased productivity, that we can reduce and, yes, eliminate inflation.

Our aim is to increase our national wealth so that all will have more, not just redistribute what we already have, which is just a sharing of scarcity. We can begin to reward hard work and risk-taking, by forcing the Government to live within its means.

Over the years, we have let negative economic forces run

out of control. We have stalled the judgement day. We no longer have that luxury. We are out of time.

And to you, my fellow citizens, let us join a new determination to rebuild the foundations of our society; to work together to act responsibly. Let us do so with the most profound respect for that which must be preserved as well as with sensitive understanding and compassion for those who must be protected.

Less than two weeks later, President Reagan addressed a joint session of Congress to deliver a "State of the Union Message on Economic Recovery."

There is nothing wrong with our internal strengths. There has been no breakdown in the human, technological and natural resources upon which the economy is built.

No administration can promise to immediately stop a trend that has grown in recent years as quickly as Government expenditures themselves. But let me say this: Waste and fraud in the Federal budget is exactly what I have called it before—an unrelenting national scandal—a scandal we are bound and determined to do something about.

We have no intention of dismantling the regulatory agencies—especially those necessary to protect the environment and to assure the public health and safety. However, we must come to grips with inefficient and burdensome regulations—eliminate those we can and reform those we must keep.

On September 24, 1981, President Reagan again addressed the American people on "Additional Reductions in Federal Spending: Our Plan for Recovery is Sound."

Shortly after taking office, I came before you to map out a four-part plan for national economic recovery:

—Tax cuts to stimulate more growth and more jobs;

—Spending cuts to put an end to continuing deficits and high inflation;

—Regulatory relief to lift the heavy burden of Government rules and paper work;

—and finally, a steady, consistent monetary policy.

We have made strong, encouraging progress on all four fronts.

But all of you know that interest rates will only come down and stay down when Government is no longer borrowing huge amounts of money to cover its deficits.

In the last few decades, we started down a road that led to a massive explosion in Federal spending. It took about 170 years for the Federal budget to reach $100 billion. That was in 1962. It only took eight years to reach the $200 billion mark and only five more years after that to make it $300 billion. In the next five, we nearly doubled that.

It would be one thing if we'd been able to pay for all the things Government decided to do, but we've only balanced the budget once in the last 20 years. In just the past decade, our national debt has more than doubled. And in the next few days, it will pass the trillion dollar mark. One trillion dollars of debt—if we as a nation need a warning, let that be it.

I believe we've chosen a path that leads to an America at work, to fiscal sanity, to lower taxes and less inflation. I believe our plan for recovery is sound and it will work.

I believe the spirit of volunteerism still lives in America. We see examples of it on every hand—the community charity drive, support of hospitals and all manner of non-profit institutions, the rallying around when disaster or tragedy strikes.

The truth is we've let Government take away many things we once considered were really ours to do voluntarily out of the goodness of our hearts and a sense of community pride and neighborliness.

I believe many of you want to do those things again, want to be involved if only someone will ask you or offer the opportunity. Well, we intend to make that offer.

We are launching a nationwide effort to encourage our citizens to join with us in finding where need exists and then to organize volunteer programs to meet that need.

We have already set the wheels of such a volunteer effort in motion.

As Tom Paine said 200 years ago: "We have it within our power to begin the world over again."

What are we waiting for?

Just five days later, President Reagan addressed the 1981 Annual Meeting of the Board of Governors of the World Bank and International Monetary Fund. His topic was "The Magic of the Market Place: We cannot have prosperity without economic freedom."

We who live in free market societies believe that growth and prosperity, and ultimately human fulfillment are created from the bottom up, not the government down.

Only when the human spirit is allowed to invent and create, only when individuals are given a personal stake in deciding economic policies and benefiting from their success—only then can societies remain economically alive, dynamic, prosperous, progressive and free.

Trust the people. This is the one irrefutable lesson of the entire postwar period contradicting the notion that rigid government controls are essential to economic development.

The societies which have achieved the most spectacular, broad-based economic programs in the shortest period of time are not the most tightly controlled, nor necessarily the biggest in size, or the wealthiest in natural resources. No, what unites them is their willingness to believe in the magic of the market place.

Every day life confirms the fundamentally human and democratic ideal that individual effort deserves economic reward. Nothing is more crushing to the spirit of the working people and to the vision of development itself than the absence of reward for honest toil and legitimate risk. So let me speak plainly: we cannot have prosperity and successful development without economic freedom. Nor can we preserve our personal and political freedoms without economic freedom.

By reducing the rate of Government spending, honoring our commitment to balance the budget, reducing tax rates to encourage productive investment and personal savings, eliminating excessive Government regulation, and maintaining a stable monetary policy, we are convinced we will enter a new era of sustained, noninflationary growth and prosperity, the likes of which we have not seen for many years.

And, as the world's largest single market, a prosperous,

growing U.S. economy will mean increased trading opportunities for other nations.

In his 1982 State of the Union Address, President Reagan gave Congress and the American people a report on the progress already made and the challenges that still lay ahead.

Together, after 50 years of taking power away from the hands of the people in their states and local communities, we have started returning power and resources to them.

And that plan is based on four common-sense fundamentals: continued reduction of the growth in Federal spending, preserving the individual and business tax reductions that will stimulate saving and investment, removing unnecessary Federal regulations to spark productivity and maintaining a healthy dollar and a stable monetary policy —the latter a responsibility of the Federal Reserve System.

Higher taxes would not mean lower deficits. If they did, how would we explain tax revenues more than doubled just since 1976, yet in that same six-year period we ran the largest series of deficits in our history?

Raising taxes won't balance the budget. It will encourage more Government spending and less private investment. Raising taxes will slow economic growth, reduce production and destroy future jobs, making it more difficult for those without jobs to find them and more likely that those who now have jobs could lose them.

So I will not ask you to try to balance the budget on the backs of the American taxpayers. I will seek no tax increases this year and I have no intention of retreating from our basic program of tax relief. I promised the American people to bring their tax rates down and keep them down—to provide them with incentives to rebuild our economy, to save, to invest in America's future. I will stand by my word. Tonight I'm urging the American people: Seize these new opportunities to produce, to save, to invest, and together we'll make this economy a mighty engine of freedom, hope and prosperity again.

Some will say our mission is to save free enterprise. Well, I say we must save free enterprise so that, together, we can save America.

I am confident the economic program we've put into operation will protect the needy while it triggers a recovery that will benefit all Americans. It will stimulate the economy, result in increased savings and provide capital for expansion, mortgages for home building and jobs for the unemployed.

Our citizens feel they've lost control of even the most basic decisions made about the essential services of Government, such as schools, welfare, roads, and even garbage collection. And they're right.

A maze of interlocking jurisdictions and levels of Government confronts average citizens in trying to solve even the simplest of problems. They don't know where to turn for answers, who to hold accountable, who to praise, who to blame, who to vote for or against.

In April, 1982, the President again went to the American people over national television to discuss the economy. He made it clear that a balanced federal budget is essential to a healthy American economy but that it is not something we will ever be able to count on Congress to do willingly and voluntarily. He felt that a balanced budget would have to be forced on Washington.

And because Government always finds a need for whatever money it gets, the cost of Government has continued to go up.

If American workers can show the statesmanship they've shown in redrawing their contracts to restrain their own wages to help in this time of recession, surely we in Washington can show some statesmanship too.

Once we've achieved a balanced budget—and we will—I want to insure that we keep it for many long years after I've left office. And there's only one way to do that. So tonight, I am asking the Congress to pass as soon as possible a constitutional amendment to require balanced Federal budgets.

Only a constitutional amendment will do the job. We've
tried the carrot and it failed. With the stick of a balanced
budget amendment, we can stop the Government's squan-
dering, overtaxing ways and save our economy.

Time and again, the American people—you—have
worked wonders that have astounded the world. We've
done it in war and peace, in good times and bad. Because
we're a people who care and who know how to pull together—family by family, community by community, coast to
coast—to change things for the better.

The success story of America is neighbor helping neighbor. So tonight, I ask for your help, your voice at this
turning point. So often in history, great causes have been
won or lost at the last moment because one side or the
other lacked that last reserve of character and stamina, of
faith and fortitude to see their way through to success.

*And, in June of that same year, when he was carrying his
message of world peace to far distant shores, President Reagan reminded the British Parliament of the importance to
controlling Government:*

At the same time, there is a threat posed to human
freedom by the enormous power of the modern state. History teaches the danger of government that overreaches:
political control takes precedence over free economic
growth; secret police, mindless bureaucracy—all combin-
ing to stifle individual excellence and personal freedom.

Now I am aware that among us here and throughout
Europe there is legitimate disagreement over the extent to
which the public sector should play a role in a nation's
economy and life. But on one point all of us are united: our
abhorrence of dictatorship in all its forms but most particularly the totalitarianism and the terrible inhumani-
ties it has caused in our time: the great purge, Auschwitz
and Dachau, the Gulag and Cambodia.

CHAPTER 7

"I pledged loyalty to only one special interest group—'We the people.' "

From his introduction to the national political scene with his "A Time for Choosing" address in 1964, through the first term of his Presidency, Ronald Reagan has always made it clear that he was preaching a "new" gospel of conservatism, of Republicanism—one that included all Americans, not just a special few.

He has remained consistent in that approach throughout his entire political career. His concern has been for all Americans, no matter the age, income, sex, race, profession or any other factor.

In 1966, when he announced his candidacy for Governor of California, Ronald Reagan described his outlook on various public assistance programs in a manner that remains unchanged today, that such programs definitely need to be maintained, but they also need to be run in such a way as to prevent flagrant abuses.

Working men and women should not be asked to carry the additional burden of a segment of society capable of caring for itself but which prefers making welfare a way of life, freeloading at the expense of the more conscientious citizens.

In 1977, Ronald Reagan spoke to the Intercollegiate Studies Institute on the subject of the new conservative movement.

The new Republican Party I envision will not, and cannot, be limited to the country club-Big Business image that for reasons both fair and unfair it is burdened with today. It is going to have room for the man and woman in the factories, for the farmer, for the cop on the beat, and the millions of Americans who may never have thought of joining our party before. If we are to attract more working men and women, we must welcome them, not only as rank-and-file members but as leaders and candidates.

I refuse to believe that the Good Lord divided this world into Republicans, who defend basic values, and Democrats, who win elections. We have to find the tough, bright young men and women who are tired of the clichés and the pomposity and the mind-numbing economic idiocy of the liberals in Washington.

When we are maligned as having little thought or compassion for people, let us denounce the slander for what it is. . . . Concern for the people is at the very heart of conservatism. Concern for the dignity of all men; that those in need shall be helped to become independent—not lifetime recipients of a dole; concern that those who labor and produce will not be robbed of the fruit of their toil or their liberty. Concern that we shall not forfeit the dream that we can become as a shining city on a hill.

Believing in that dream, I became a Republican and because of that dream, I am a conservative.

When he accepted his party's nomination as their Presidential candidate, Ronald Reagan made it apparent to those assembled in Detroit and elsewhere that his campaign would be directed at all Americans

More than anything else, I want my candidacy to unify our country; to renew the American spirit and sense of purpose. I want to carry our message to every American, regardless of party affiliation, who is a member of this community of shared values.

It is essential that we maintain both the forward momentum of economic growth and the strength of the safety net between those in our society who need help. We also believe it is essential that the integrity of all aspects of Social Security be preserved.

When those in leadership give us tax increases and tell us we must also do with less, have they thought about those who've always had less—especially the minorities? This is like telling them that just as they step on the first rung of the ladder of opportunity, the ladder is being pulled out from under them. That may be the Democratic leadership's message to the minorities, but it won't be our message. Ours, ours will be: We have to move ahead, but we're not going to leave anyone behind.

It's time to put America back to work, to make our cities and towns resound with the confident voices of men and women of all races, nationalities and faiths bringing home to their families a paycheck they can cash for honest money.

For those without skills, we'll find a way to help them get new skills.

For those without job opportunities, we'll stimulate new opportunities, especially in the inner cities where they live.

For those who've abandoned hope, we'll restore hope and we'll welcome them into a great national crusade to make America great again.

In that acceptance speech, he also specifically addressed the question of sexual discrimination.

As President, I will establish a liaison with the 50 Governors to encourage them to eliminate wherever it exists, discrimination against women. I will monitor Federal laws to insure their implementation and to add statutes if they are needed.

Early in the 1980 Presidential campaign, Ronald Reagan was pressed for his view on whether America's economic condition was more aptly termed a recession or a depression. He used his concern for the people to reply.

As far as I am concerned, the line between recession and depression cannot be measured in the strict economists' terms but must be measured in human terms. When our working people—including those who are unemployed—must endure the worst misery since the 1930s, then I think we ought to recognize that they consider it a depression.

And in a September 1980 campaign speech to the International Business Council in Chicago, Ronald Reagan made it clear that in his efforts to restore the economy, he was not about to sacrifice entitlement programs for those deserving of such entitlements.

This strategy for growth does not require altering or

taking back necessary entitlements already granted to the American people. The integrity of the Social Security system will be defended by my administration and its benefits will once again be made meaningful.

In an October 1980 press conference, candidate Reagan answered a reporter's question with a statement that caused considerable commotion but which proved one of his most prophetic.

One of the first Supreme Court vacancies in my administration will be filled by the most qualified woman I can find.

In his Presidential Inaugural Address, Ronald Reagan again reminded the American people that his concern and the concern of his entire administration was for all Americans, "We the People."

We hear much of special-interest groups. Well, our concern must be for a special-interest group that has long been neglected. It knows no sectional boundaries or ethnic or racial divisions and it crosses party lines. It is made up of men and women who raise our food, patrol our streets, man our mines and factories, teach our children, keep our homes and heal us when we're sick. Professional, industrialists, shopkeepers, cabbies and truck drivers. They are, in short, "we the people." This breed called Americans.

Well, this Administration's objective will be a healthy, vigorous, growing economy that provides equal opportunities for all Americans with no barriers born of bigotry or discrimination.

Putting America back to work means putting all Americans back to work. Ending inflation means freeing all Americans from the terror of runaway living costs.

All must share in the productive work of this "new beginning," and all must share in the bounty of a revived economy.

Those who say that we're in a time when there are no heroes—they just don't know where to look. You can see heroes every day going in and out of factory gates. Others, a handful in number, produce enough food to feed all of us and the world beyond.

You meet heroes across a counter—and they're on both sides of that counter. There are entrepreneurs with faith in themselves and faith in an idea who create new jobs, new wealth and opportunity.

There are individuals and families whose taxes support the Government and whose voluntary gifts support church, charity, culture, art and education. Their patriotism is quiet but deep. Their values sustain our national life.

Now, I have used the words "they" and "their" in speaking of these heroes. I could say "you" and "your" because I'm addressing the heroes of whom I speak—you the citizens of this blessed land.

How can we love our country and not love our countrymen? And loving them reach out a hand when they fall, heal them when they're sick and provide opportunity to make them self-sufficient so they will be equal in fact and not just in theory?

Throughout the campaign and even after Ronald Reagan took office, there were a constant string of accusations that his proposed economic reforms would cause undue suffering among those dependent on public assistance programs, including Social Security. Very soon after his inauguration, President Reagan, in a televised address, "The State of the Nation's Economy," sought to correct false impressions.

Our spending cuts will not be at the expense of the truly needy. We will, however, seek to eliminate benefits to those who are not really qualified by reason of need.

Our basic system is sound. We can, with compassion, continue to meet our responsibility to those who through no fault of their own need our help. We can meet fully the other legitimate responsibilities of Government. We cannot continue any longer our wasteful ways at the expense of the workers of this land or our children.

Less than two weeks later, the President delivered a "State of the Union Message on Economic Recovery" to a joint session of Congress. He sought, in that address, to

meet head on some of the false impressions that were being
circulated.

Some of you have heard from constituents afraid that
Social Security checks, for example, might be taken from
them. I regret the fear these unfounded stories have raised
and welcome this opportunity to set things straight.

We will continue to fulfill the obligations that spring
from our national conscience. Those who through no fault
of their own must depend on the rest of us, the poverty-
stricken, the disabled, the elderly, all those with true need,
can rest assured that the social safety net of programs they
depend on are exempt from any cuts.

The full retirement benefits of the more than 31 million
Social Security recipients will be continued along with an
annual cost of living increase. Medicare will not be cut, nor
will supplemental income for the blind, aged and disabled.
Funding will continue for veterans' pensions.

School breakfasts and lunches for the children of low-
income families will continue as will nutrition and other
special services for the aging. There will be no cut in Project Head Start or summer youth jobs.

All in all, nearly $216 billion providing help for tens of
millions of Americans will be fully funded. But Government will not continue to subsidize individuals or particular business interests where real need cannot be
demonstrated.

The Food Stamp Program will be restored to its original
purpose, to assist those without resources to purchase
sufficient nutritional food.

We will, however, save $1.8 billion in Fiscal Year 1982
by removing from eligibility those who are not in real need
or who are abusing the program. Despite this reduction,
the program will be budgeted for more than $10 billion.

We will tighten welfare and give more attention to outside sources of income when determining the amount of
welfare an individual is allowed. This plus strong and
effective work requirements will save $520 million next
year.

I stated a moment ago our intention to keep the school
breakfast and lunch programs for those in need. But by
cutting back on meals for children of families that can

afford to pay, the savings will be $1.6 billion in Fiscal Year 1982.

I hope I've made it plain that our approach has been even-handed; that only the programs for the truly needy remain untouched.

Appearing once again before a Joint Session of Congress in April, 1981, President Reagan spoke of the growing impatience of the American people.

When I took the oath of office, I pledged loyalty to only one special interest group—"We, the People." Those people—neighbors and friends, shopkeepers and laborers, farmers and craftsmen—do not have infinite patience. As a matter of fact, some 80 years ago, Theodore Roosevelt wrote these instructive words in his first message to the Congress: "The American people are slow to wrath, but when their wrath is once kindled, it burns like a consuming flame."

Well, perhaps that kind of wrath will be deserved if our answer to these serious problems is to repeat the mistakes of the past. The old and comfortable way is to shave a little here and add a little there. Well, that's not acceptable any more. I think this great and historic Congress knows that way is no longer acceptable.

On May 27, 1981, President Reagan delivered the commencement address at the United States Military Academy and delivered his message of the supreme importance of the American people—men and women.

We've been through a period in which it seemed that we, the people, had forgotten that government is a convenience of, for and by the people.

General George Patton said, "Wars may be fought with weapons, but they are won by men." It is the spirit of the men who follow and of the man who leads that gains the victory. Now today we seek only to make one change in that statement: It is "the men and women who follow" and the "men and women who lead."

Later, in July, President Reagan addressed the American people once again on the matter of the economy and

*once again reassured Social Security recipients of his con-
cern for their continued well-being.*

I've been deeply disturbed by the way those of you who
are dependent on Social Security have been needlessly
frightened by some of the inaccuracies which have been
given wide circulation.

It's true that the Social Security system has financial
problems. It is also true that these financial problems have
been building for more than 20 years—and nothing has
been done.

I hope to address you on this entire subject in the near
future. In the meantime, let me just say this: I will not
stand by and see those of you who are dependent on Social
Security deprived of the benefits you've worked so hard to
earn. I make that pledge to you as your President. You
have no reason to be frightened. You will continue to receive your checks in the full amount due you. In any plan
to restore fiscal integrity to Social Security, I will personally see that the plan will not be at the expense of you who
are now dependent on your monthly Social Security
checks.

*In a September 1981 address to the American people, on
additional reductions in federal spending, President Reagan reiterated his position that, even in Social Security,
those not truly in need could not depend on being taken care
of at the expense of those who are fully dependent on Social
Security—the same approach he has always taken to other
entitlement programs.*

I am asking the Congress to restore the minimum benefit for current beneficiaries with low incomes. It was
never our intention to take this support away from those
who truly need it.

There is, however, a sizable percentage of recipients who
are adequately provided for by pensions or other income
and should not be adding to the financial burden of Social
Security.

The same situation prevails with regard to disability
payments. No one will deny our obligation to those with
legitimate claims. But there is widespread abuse of the
system which should not be allowed to continue.

I cannot and will not stand by and see financial hardship

imposed on the more than 36 million senior citizens who
have worked and served this nation throughout their lives.
They deserve better from us.

*Just five days later, the President addressed the Annual
Meeting of the Board of Governors of the World Bank and
the International Monetary Fund. He told his audience
that for any nation to prosper, that prosperity must origi-
nate with the people.*

We who live in free market societies believe that growth,
prosperity, and ultimately human fulfillment, are created
from the bottom up, not the government down.

Only when the human spirit is allowed to invent and
create, only when individuals are given a personal stake
in deciding economic policies and benefiting from their
success—only then can societies remain economically
alive, dynamic, prosperous, progressive and free.

*In his 1982 State of the Union Message, President Rea-
gan devoted considerable time to his concern for all Americans.*

What we do and say here will make all the difference to
auto workers in Detroit, lumberjacks in the Northwest,
steelworkers in Steubenville who are in the unemployment lines, to black teen-agers in Newark and Chicago; to
hard-pressed farmers and small businessmen and to millions of everyday Americans who harbor the simple wish
of a safe and financially secure future for their children.

Contrary to some of the wild charges you may have
heard, this Administration has not and will not turn its
back on America's elderly or America's poor. Under the
new budget, funding for social insurance programs will be
more than double the amount spent only six years ago.

But it would be foolish to pretend that these or any
programs cannot be made more efficient and economical.

The entitlement programs that make up our safety net
for the truly needy have worthy goals and many deserving
recipients. We will protect them. But there's only one way
to see to it that these programs really help those whom
they were designed to help, and that is to bring their spiraling costs under control.

Well, something is going to happen. Not only the taxpayers are defrauded—the people with real dependency on these programs are deprived of what they need because available resources are going not to the needy but to the greedy.

But don't be fooled by those who proclaim that spending cuts will deprive the elderly, the needy and the helpless. The Federal Government will still subsidize 95 million meals every day. That's one out of seven of all the meals served in America. Head Start, senior nutrition programs, and child welfare programs will not be cut from the levels we proposed last year. More than one-half billion dollars has been proposed for minority business assistance. And research at the National Institutes of Health will be increased by over $100 million. While meeting all these needs, we intend to plug unwarranted tax loopholes and strengthen the law which requires all large corporations to pay a minimum tax.

We don't have to turn to our history books for heroes. They're all around us. One who sits among you here tonight epitomized that heroism at the end of the longest imprisonment ever inflicted on men of our armed forces. Who will ever forget that night when we waited for television to bring us the scene of that first plane landing at Clark Field in the Philippines—bringing our P.O.W.s home. The plane door opened and Jeremiah Denton came slowly down the ramp. He caught sight of our flag, saluted it, said "God Bless America," and then thanked us for bringing him home.

Just two weeks ago, in the midst of a terrible tragedy on the Potomac, we saw again the spirit of American heroism at its finest—the heroism of dedicated rescue workers saving crash victims from icy waters. And we saw the heroism of one of our young Government employees, Lenny Skutnik, who, when he saw a woman lose her grip on the helicopter line, dived into the water and dragged her to safety.

And then there are the countless quiet, everyday heroes of American life—parents who sacrifice long and hard so their children will know a better life than they've known; church and civic volunteers who help to feed, clothe, nurse and teach the needy; millions who've made our nation, and our nation's destiny, so very special—unsung heroes who may not have realized their own dreams themselves but then who reinvest those dreams in their children.

President Reagan used the occasion of his 1983 State of the Union Message to announce a solution to the problems of Social Security and to make it clearer than ever that not only would his Administration not cater to any privileged groups at the expense of any others, it would not tolerate any attempts to do so by others.

When the Speaker of the House, the Senate Majority Leader and I formed the bipartisan Commission on Social Security, pundits and experts predicted that party divisions and conflicting interests would prevent the Commission from agreeing on a plan to save Social Security.

Well, sometimes, even here in Washington, the cynics are wrong. Through compromise and cooperation, the members of the Commission overcame their differences and achieved a fair, workable plan. They proved that, when it comes to the national welfare, Americans can still pull together for the common good.

Tonight, I am especially pleased to join with the Speaker and the Senate majority leader in urging the Congress to enact this plan within the next hundred days.

There are elements in it, of course, that none of us prefers, but taken together it forms a package all of us can support. It asks for some sacrifice by all—the self-employed, beneficiaries, workers, new Government employees, and the better-off among the retired—but it imposes an undue burden on none. And, in supporting it, we keep an important pledge to the American people: the integrity of the Social Security system will be preserved—and no one's payment will be reduced.

No domestic challenge is more crucial than providing stable, permanent jobs for all Americans who want to work.

Our commitment to fairness means that we must assure legal and economic equity for women, and eliminate, once and for all, all traces of unjust discrimination against women from the U.S. Code. We will not tolerate wage discrimination based on sex and we intend to strengthen enforcement of child support laws to insure that single parents, most of whom are women, do not suffer unfair financial hardship. We will also take action to remedy inequities in pensions. These initiatives will be joined by others to continue our effort to promote equality for women.

Also in the area of fairness and equity, we will ask for extension of the Civil Rights Commission, which is due to expire this year. The Commission is an important part of the ongoing struggle for justice in America, and we strongly support its reauthorization. Effective enforcement of our nation's fair housing laws is also essential to insuring equal opportunity. In the year ahead, we will work to strengthen enforcement of fair housing laws for all Americans.

On August 26, 1983, President Reagan addressed the Republican Women's Leadership Forum in San Diego. He reminded those in attendance of the record of his administration in recognizing and appointing capable women to positions of importance, but assured them that it was only a beginning.

And just look at the record. For the first time in history, three women serve in the Cabinet of the United States, Secretary Dole, Secretary Heckler and Ambassador Kirkpatrick.

We've also appointed more women to top policy-making positions in our first two years than any previous administration has in a similar period. We've appointed more than 1,200 women to executive positions throughout the government. And while that record is better than our predecessors, it's only a beginning. And of course, on another beginning, I'm proud to say we appointed the first woman to the Supreme Court.

What all this adds up to is clear: The greatest political opportunity for women in this country, real progress, rather than words and promises, rests with the Republican Party.

CHAPTER 8

"You and I have a rendezvous with history."

Ronald Reagan is keenly aware of history, both in the sense of Americans in the 1980s looking back on the actions of our forefathers and the legacy they left us, and in the sense of Americans generations from now looking back on our actions today—and the legacy we leave them.

That perspective was stated so vividly in "A Time for Choosing."

You and I have a rendezvous with history. We will preserve for our children this, the last best hope for man on earth or we will sentence them to take the last step into a thousand years of darkness. If we fail, at least let our children, and our children's children, say of us we justified our brief moment here. We did all that could be done.

And elsewhere in that speech, he reminded us in a different fashion how we would be remembered for what we do, or fail to do, today.

We are at war with the most dangerous enemy that has ever faced mankind in his long climb from the swamp to the stars, and it has been said if we lose that war, and in so doing, lose this way of freedom of ours, history will record with the greatest astonishment that those who had the most to lose did the least to prevent its happening.

In 1976, Ronald Reagan addressed the Republican National Convention after Gerald Ford's acceptance speech. Urging everyone to work together harder than ever before, he also spoke of the reactions of Americans a century later.

Whether they have the freedom that we have known up until now will depend on what we do here. Will they look back with appreciation and say, "Thank God for those people in 1976 who headed off that loss of freedom, who kept us now a hundred years later free, who kept our world from nuclear destruction"? This is our challenge. And this is why we've got to quit talking to each other and about each other and go out and communicate to the world that we may be fewer in numbers than we've ever been, but we carry the message they're waiting for. We must go forth from here united, determined, believing what a great general said a few years ago. "There is no substitute for victory."

In his acceptance speech at the Republican Convention four years later, Ronald Reagan expressed concern over the message the Democratic leadership would have us give our children.

They expect you to tell your children that the American people no longer have the will to cope with their problems; that the future will be one of sacrifice and few opportunities.

In his Inaugural Address, President Reagan said it most succinctly:

We must act today in order to preserve tomorrow.

Shortly after taking office, the President addressed the nation on "The State of the Union's Economy." He told us the choice of what we leave for our children is up to us.

We can leave our children with an unrepayable massive debt and a shattered economy or we can leave them liberty in a land where every individual has the opportunity to be whatever God intended us to be. All it takes is a little common sense and recognition of our own ability. Together we can forge a new beginning for America.

Later in 1981, the President addressed the graduating class at West Point. He reminded them of the depth of their obligation:

Do your duty. Keep untarnished your honor, and you of the corps will preserve this country for yourselves, for all of us, for your children and for your children's children.

President Reagan's 1982 State of the Union Message contained some of the most memorable passages about our obligations to those who will follow us.

The record is clear, and I believe that history will remember this as an era of American renewal, remember this Administration as an Administration of change and remember this Congress as a Congress of destiny.

One hundred and twenty years ago, the greatest of all our Presidents delivered his second State of the Union message in this chamber. "We cannot escape history," Abraham Lincoln warned. "We of this Congress and this Administration will be remembered in spite of ourselves." The "trial through which we pass will light us down in honor or dishonor to the latest generation."

Well, that President and that Congress did not fail the American people. Together, they weathered the storm and preserved the union.

Let it be said of us that we, too, did not fail; that we, too, worked together to bring America through difficult times. Let us so conduct ourselves that two centuries from now, another Congress and another President, meeting in this chamber as we're meeting, will speak of us with pride, saying that we met the test and preserved for them in their day the sacred flame of liberty—this last, best hope of man on earth.

In June 1982, President Reagan addressed the British Parliament in London. He told them of his plans and goals for peace throughout the world, not just for ourselves . . .

The task I have set forth will long outlive our own generation. But together, we, too have come through the worst. Let us now begin a major effort to secure the best—a crusade for freedom that will engage the faith and fortitude of the next generation. For the sake of peace and justice, let us move toward a world in which all people are at last free to determine their own destiny.

Just over a week later, in addressing the United Nations Second Special Session on Disarmament, President Reagan told those assembled:

With God's help, we can secure life and freedom for generations to come.

President Reagan told the 1982 graduating class from

his alma mater, Eureka College, that his mission as President of the United States was to attempt to unify the free world in the quest for the greatest goal of all.

I believe that the West can fashion a realistic, durable policy that will protect our interests and keep the peace, not just for this generation, but for your children and grandchildren.

Addressing the American people on the subject of Arms Control, and the MX Missile, the President spoke reassuringly of the legacy he'd like to leave the next generation.

Our children should not grow up frightened. They should not fear the future. We're working to make it peaceful and free. I believe their future can be the brightest, most exciting of any generation. We must reassure them and let them know that their parents and the leaders of this world are seeking, above all else, to keep them safe and at peace. I consider this to be a sacred trust.

In his 1983 State of the Union Message, President Reagan expressed his concern for the world we would leave our children, but also how they would view our actions.

To assure a sustained recovery, we must continue getting runaway spending under control to bring those deficits down. If we do not, the recovery will be too short, unemployment will remain too high, and we will leave an unconscionable burden of national debt for our children. That we must not do.

If we do that, if we care what our children and our children's children will say of us, if we want them one day to be thankful for what we did here in these temples of freedom, we will work together to make America better for our having been here—not just in this year, or in this decade, but in the next century and beyond.

In his March 23, 1983, address to the nation in which he proposed a bold new departure in our nation's defense strategy, including the deployment of spaceborne, nonnuclear systems to defend against nuclear missiles, the President once again made it clear his decision to take this action was not merely limited to protection for those of us alive today.

The subject I want to discuss with you tonight, peace and national security, is both timely and important—timely because I have reached a decision which offers a new hope for our children in the 21st century.

CHAPTER 9

"Status Quo.
That's latin for 'the mess we're in.' "

Ronald Reagan has always had a great fondness for humor and is blessed with a marvelous, quick, sense of humor himself. His career is full of examples of his sharp wit, his ability to laugh and, perhaps the greatest gift of all, his willingness to laugh at himself.

He has used humor merely as an ice-breaker, he has used it to relieve incredible tension, and he has used it to make points that could not have been so clearly made otherwise.

A campaign favorite came up whenever Candidate Reagan was pressed on whether America was going through a recession, a depression, or what. He would reply.

If he (President Carter) wants a definition, I'll give him one. A recession is when your neighbor loses his job. A depression is when you lose yours. And recovery is when Jimmy Carter loses his.

Back in the beginning of his political career, Ronald Reagan used humor in "A Time for Choosing," in 1964, to make points that he would continue to make throughout public life.

A government agency is the nearest thing to eternal life we'll ever see on this earth.

And

There are now two and one half million Federal employees. No one knows what they all do. One Congressman found out what one of them does. This man sits at a desk in Washington. Documents come to him each morning. He reads them, initials them, and passes them on to the proper agency. One day a document arrived that he wasn't supposed to read, but he read it, initialled it and passed it on. Twenty four hours later it arrived back at his desk with a memo attached that said, "You weren't supposed to read this. Erase your initials and initial the erasure."

Ronald Reagan was sworn in as Governor of California at 16 minutes past midnight on January 2, 1967. With his good friend from Hollywood, U.S. Senator George Murphy with him and a full battery of television cameras, Governor Reagan turned to his friend and said:

Well, here we are on the late show again.

Humor became a standard ingredient throughout Ronald Reagan's campaign for the presidency. While dealing with crucial issues like peace through strength and economic recovery for all Americans, Reagan's wit served him well, suggesting to the American people that he was something other than the ogre the opposition had been depicting.

Examples of his campaign humor are countless. A few:

Status Quo—that's Latin for "the mess we're in."

Herbert Hoover was the first President to return his entire salary to the Government. Now we're all doing it.

The difference between them (the Democrats) and us (the Republicans) is that we want to check government spending and they want to spend government checks.

Hearing President Carter and members of his administration use the language of free enterprise reminds me of one of the stories of Mark Twain. He had a habit of using very foul language which distressed his wife to no end. She decided on a form of shock treatment to cure him of his habit. One day he came home, and she stood in front of him and recited every word of the salty language she had ever heard him use. He listened patiently and when she was finished, said: "My dear, you have the words all right, you just don't have the tune."

An issue that obviously proved to be a non-issue during the campaign was Ronald Reagan's age. But so many tried to make so much of it, that, ever since, President Reagan has gotten a lot of mileage, and a lot of laughs, by joking about his own age.

Shortly after his inauguration, he addressed the National Press Club.

I know your organization was founded by six Washington newspaperwomen in 1919 . . . seems only yesterday.

Middle age is when you're faced with two temptations and you choose the one that gets you home by 9 o'clock.

And he quoted Thomas Jefferson to them:

He said that one should not worry about one's exact chronological age in reference to his ability to perform one's task. And ever since he told me that . . .

Observing George Bush's 57th birthday in April, 1981, the then 70-year-old President said:

We have a great relationship, and George was very tactful—he hasn't told me how young he is.

In his address to the U.S. Military Academy at West Point in May, 1981:

I'm a little self-conscious being introduced as your commander, when I began my military career as a second lieutenant in the cavalry—the horse cavalry that is. I have threatened on occasion that that was the reason I got this job, so that I could reinstitute that horse cavalry.

At the same time, I accept without question the words of George Washington: To be prepared for war is one of the most effectual means of preserving the peace.
Now, in spite of some of the things you may have heard, he didn't tell me that personally.

George Washington came up again with reference to his age in his 1982 State of the Union message.

Today marks my first State of the Union address to you, a constitutional duty as old as our republic itself.
President Washington began this tradition in 1790 after reminding the nation that the destiny of self-government and the "preservation of the sacred fire of liberty" is "finally staked on the experiment entrusted to the hands of the American people." For our friends in the press, who place a high premium in accuracy, let me say: I did not personal-

ly hear George Washington say that, but it is a matter of historic record.

After his election, President-elect Reagan was undergoing a pre-inauguration briefing by a team of foreign policy advisers on various problems throughout the world. As the briefing went on, he finally said:

I think I'll demand a recount!

He must have been paying attention to them however. Later, when critics were describing the President's approach to foreign policy as too simplistic, he issued this stern warning to the Soviet Union:

Roses are red, violets are blue. Stay out of El Salvador, and Poland, too.

In a similar vein, facing growing opposition to his support of the B-1 bomber, President Reagan used humor to divert some of the criticism.

How did I know it was an airplane? I thought it was vitamins for the troops.

The President's aides and Cabinet members have not escaped unscathed, either.

During a White House ribbon cutting ceremony, the President waved the scissors with a flourish and said:

I've been practicing all morning on Ed Meese's tie.

Ed was the subject again during a later session at Camp David.

The first time I came to this place, Ed Meese sewed name tags on all my undershorts and T-shirts.

While James Watt was still Secretary of the Interior, the President used to tell the story of an environmentalist who had finally found a new, sure way to make his children behave:

He now scares them into being good by telling them James Watt will get them.

And Budget Director Dave Stockman, who has been instrumental in administering most of the President's belt-tightening measures.

I was discussing our belt-tightening measures with President Ford, while we were also talking about his new library and museum back in Michigan. I found myself very envious of him. I came back—and with an eye on the future—I spoke to Dave Stockman about that subject. He tells me he's been pricing bookmobiles.

The President obviously enjoys college commencement exercises. At West Point, he tried to prepare the graduates for their Army careers.

I doubt there will be many surprises because, in a way, you've been "Army" for the last four years. There's little chance that you'll be like the recruit in World War II, who asked in some bewilderment why the Army did certain things in the way that it did. A longtime Army sergeant said, "Well, let me explain it to you son. If you were in charge of a brand new country and in creating an army for that country, you finally got a division organized, what would you call it?" The recruit thought for a minute and said, "Well, I guess I'd call it the First Division." "Well," he said, "in the United States Army, when they did that, they called it the Second Division." And he said, "When you understand that, you'll know everything about the Army and why it does things."

A year later, he addressed the graduating class at his alma mater, Eureka College.

Over the years since I sat where you of the graduating class of 1982 are now sitting, I've returned to the campus many times, always with great pleasure and warm nostalgia. It isn't true that I just came back to clean out my locker in the gym.

On one of those occasions, I addressed a graduating class here, " 'neath the elms," and was awarded an honorary degree. I informed those assembled that while I was grateful for the honor, it added to a feeling of guilt I'd been nursing for 25 years. I always figured the first degree I was given was honorary.

The President has a couple of favorite stories he likes to tell to make points about his belief in restoring the volunteer spirit in America.

One of them deals with the chairman of a small town

charity drive who approached a very wealthy citizen to ask for a contribution.

He told him the town records showed that he never contributed any money for the annual charity. The prominent citizen asked, "do the records also show that I have a widowed mother who was left destitute, an older brother who was totally disabled in the war, and a sister with four children whose husband left her with no means?" The abashed citizen said, "Well, no, our records don't show that." The prominent citizen answered, "Well, I don't give any money to them so why should I give it to you?"

The other is a story of an elderly American tourist in Italy, obviously unimpressed with the story being told by his guide about a fiery volcano:

Finally, the old boy turned to his wife and said, "We got a volunteer fire department at home—put that thing out in 15 minutes."

Speaking to a group of reporters at the newly-decorated White House Press Room, the President reminded the assembled press representatives that the room is built over what used to be a swimming pool. He then remarked, although I'm not certain that some of them believed him:

Now it isn't true, however, that the floor has been hinged and can be sprung like a trap.

During a speech in Canada, President Reagan found himself frequently interrupted by anti-American hecklers. Prime Minister Pierre Trudeau was visibly embarrassed by the incidents. President Reagan attempted to ease the embarrassment by suggesting to Trudeau:

They (the hecklers) must have been imported to make me feel at home.

But at no point in his career has the President's wit been more apparent, and more welcome, than in the period immediately following the assassination attempt outside the Washington Hilton. He unleashed a string of one-liners that would have made any comedian envious.
On seeing his lovely wife, Nancy:

Honey, I forgot to duck.

Looking at the team of surgeons about to operate on him:

Please tell me you're all Republicans.

Following his surgery, President Reagan had tubes in his throat that kept him from talking. Undaunted, he put pencil and pad to good use.
One note read:

If I'd gotten this much attention in Hollywood, I would not have left.

Upon being told that a nurse would spend the night in his recovery room, he wrote:

Does Nancy know?

Another note read:

As Winnie Churchill said, "There is no more exhilarating feeling than being shot at without results."

After a particularly painful procedure, he wrote, quoting W.C. Fields:

All in all, I'd rather be in Philadelphia.

When he could talk again, he told his daughter, Maureen:

One of my new suits is ruined.

Told by a nurse that he was recovering nicely and to keep up the good work, President Reagan asked:

You mean this may happen several more times?

In a meeting with aides, he asked:

Who's minding the store?

And he told them:

I guess I really screwed up the schedule today.

When one of those aides tried to reassure him by telling the President he'd be happy to learn that the Government was running smoothly in his absence, he responded:

What makes you think I'd be happy about that?

Told that he would be unable to throw out the first ball in the major league baseball opener, he argued:

I am a right-hander, and it is the left side that hurts.

But probably my own favorite Ronald Reagan one-liner, one that expresses a sentiment very dear to my own heart, came during an interview for the Washington Star *in which the President was asked what he thought he might have done differently during the first six months of his administration.*

I wouldn't have gone to the Hilton Hotel.

Amen.

Acceptance Address
Presidential Nomination
Republican National Convention
Detroit, Michigan, July 17, 1980

Thank you very much. We're using up prime time. Thank you very much. You're singing our song. Well, the first thrill tonight was to find myself for the first time in a long time in a movie on prime time.

But this, as you can imagine, is the second big thrill.

Mr. Chairman, Mr. Vice President-to-be, this convention, my fellow citizens of this great nation:

With a deep awareness of the responsibility conferred by your trust, I accept your nomination for the Presidency of the United States. I do so with deep gratitude. And I think also I might interject on behalf of all of us our thanks to Detroit and the people of Michigan and this city for the warm hospitality we've enjoyed.

And I thank you for your wholehearted response to my recommendation in regard to George Bush as the candidate for Vice President.

I'm very proud of our party tonight. This convention has shown to all America a party united, with positive programs for solving the nation's problems; a party ready to build a new consensus with all those across the land who share a community of values embodied in these words: family, work, neighborhood, peace and freedom.

Now I know we've had a quarrel or two but only as to the method of attaining a goal. There was no argument here about the goal. As President, I will establish a liaison with the 50 Governors to encourage them to eliminate, wherever it exists, discrimination against women. I will monitor Federal laws to insure their implementation and to add statutes if they are needed.

More than anything else I want my candidacy to unify our country; to renew the American spirit and sense of purpose. I want to carry our message to every American, regardless of party affiliation, who is a member of this community of shared values.

Never before in our history have Americans been called upon to face three grave threats to our very existence, any one of which could destroy us. We face a disintegrating economy, a weakened defense and an energy policy based on the sharing of scarcity.

The major issue of this campaign is the direct political, personal, and moral responsibility of Democratic Party leadership—in the White House and in the Congress—for this unprecedented calamity which has befallen us. They tell us they've done the most that humanly could be done. They say that the United States has had its day in the sun, that our nation has passed its zenith. They expect you to tell your children that the American people no longer have the will to cope with their problems; that the future will be one of sacrifice and few opportunities.

My fellow citizens, I utterly reject that view. The American people, the most generous on earth, who created the highest standard of living, are not going to accept the notion that we can only make a better world for others by moving backward ourselves. And those who believe we can have no business leading this nation.

I will not stand by and watch this great country destroy itself under mediocre leadership that drifts from one crisis to the next, eroding our national will and purpose. We have come together here because the American people deserve better from those to whom they entrust our nation's highest offices and we stand united in our resolve to do something about it.

We need a rebirth of the American tradition of leadership at every level of government and in private life as well. The United States of America is unique in world history because it has a genius for leaders—many leaders —on many levels.

But back in 1976, Mr. Carter said, "Trust me." And a lot of people did. And now, many of those people are out of work. Many have seen their savings eaten away by inflation. Many others on fixed incomes, especially the elderly, have watched helplessly as the cruel tax of inflation wasted away their purchasing power. And, today, a great many who trusted Mr. Carter wonder if we can survive the Carter policies of national defense.

"Trust me" government asks that we concentrate our hopes and dreams in one man; that we trust him to do what's best for us. But my view of government places trust not in one person or one party, but in those values that transcend persons and parties. The trust is where it belongs—in the people. The responsibility to live up to that trust is where it belongs, in their elected leaders. That kind of relationship, between the people and their elected leaders, is a special kind of compact.

Three-hundred-and-sixty years ago, in 1620, a group of families dared to cross a mighty ocean to build a future for themselves in a new world. When they arrived at Plymouth, Massachusetts, they formed what they called a "compact," an agreement among themselves to build a community and abide by its laws.

This single act—the voluntary binding together of free people to live under the law—set the pattern for what was to come.

A century and a half later, the descendants of those people pledged their lives, their fortunes, and their sacred honor to found this nation. Some forfeited their fortunes and their lives; none sacrificed honor.

Four score and seven years later, Abraham Lincoln called upon the people of all America to renew their dedication and their commitment to a government of, for and by the people.

Isn't it once again time to renew our compact of freedom; to pledge to each other all that is best in our lives; all that gives meaning to them—for the sake of this, our beloved and blessed land?

Together, let us make this a new beginning. Let us make a commitment to care for the needy; to teach our children the virtues handed down to us by our families; to have the courage to defend those values and virtues and the willingness to sacrifice for them.

Let us pledge to restore, in our time, the American spirit of voluntary service, of cooperation, of private and community initiative; a spirit that flows like a deep and mighty river through the history of our nation.

As your nominee, I pledge to you to restore to the Federal Government the capacity to do the people's work without dominating their lives. I pledge to you a Government that will not only work well but wisely, its ability to act tempered by prudence, and its willingness to do good balanced by the knowledge that government is never more dangerous than when our desire to have it help us blinds us to its great power to harm us.

You know, the first Republican President once said, "While the people retain their virtue and their vigilance, no Administration by any extreme of wickedness or folly can seriously injure the Government in the short space of four years."

If Mr. Lincoln could see what's happened in these last three and a half years, he might hedge a little on that statement. But with the virtues that are our legacy as a free people and with the vigilance that sustains liberty, we still have time to use our renewed compact to overcome the injuries that have been done to America these past three and a half years.

First, we must overcome something the present Administration has cooked up; a new and altogether indigestible economic stew, one part inflation, one part high unemployment, one part recession, one part runaway taxes, one part deficit spending seasoned with an energy crisis. It's an economic stew that has turned the national stomach.

Ours are not problems of abstract economic theory. These are problems of flesh and blood; problems that cause pain and destroy the moral fiber of real people who should not further the indignity of being told by the Government that it is all somehow their fault. We do not have inflation —as Mr. Carter says—we've lived too well.

The head of a Government which has utterly refused to live within its means and which has, in the last few days, told us that this coming year's deficit will be $60 billion, dares to point the finger of blame at business and labor, both of which have been engaged in a losing struggle just trying to stay even.

High taxes, we are told, are somehow good for us, as if, when government spends our money it isn't inflationary, but when we spend it, it is.

Those who preside over the worst energy shortage in our history tell us to use less, so that we will run out of oil, gasoline and natural gas a little more slowly. Well, now, conservation is desirable, of course, but we must not waste energy. But conservation is not the sole answer to our energy needs.

America must get to work producing more energy. The Republican program for solving economic problems is based on growth and productivity.

Large amounts of oil and natural gas lay beneath our land and off our shores, untouched because the present Administration seems to believe the American people would rather see more regulation, more taxes and more controls than more energy.

Coal offers a great potential. So does nuclear energy produced under rigorous safety standards. It could supply electricity for thousands of industries and millions of jobs and homes. It must not be thwarted by a tiny minority opposed to economic growth which often finds friendly ears in regulatory agencies for its obstructionist campaigns.

Now make no mistake. We will not permit the safety of our people or our environmental heritage to be jeopardized, but we are going to reaffirm that the economic prosperity of our people is a fundamental part of our environment.

Our problems are both acute and chronic, yet all we hear from those in positions of leadership are the same tired proposals for more Government tinkering, more meddling and more control—all of which led us to this sorry state in the first place.

Can anyone look at the record of this Administration and say, "Well done"? Can anyone compare the state of our economy when the Carter Administration took office with where we are today and say, "Keep up the good work"? Can anyone look at our reduced standing in the world today and say, "Let's have four more years of this"?

I believe the American people are going to answer these questions, as you've answered them, in the first week of November and their answer will be, "No—we've had enough." And then it will be up to us—beginning next January 20—to offer an Administration and Congressional leadership of competence and more than a little courage.

We must have the clarity of vision to see the difference between what is essential and what is merely desirable;

and then the courage to bring our Government back under control.

It is essential that we maintain both the forward momentum of economic growth and the strength of the safety net between those in our society who need help. We also believe it is essential that the integrity of all aspects of Social Security be preserved.

Beyond these essentials, I believe it is clear our Federal Government is overgrown and overweight. Indeed, it is time our Government should go on a diet. Therefore, my first act as chief executive will be to impose an immediate and thorough freeze on Federal hiring. Then, we are going to enlist the very best minds from business, labor and whatever quarter to conduct a detailed review of every department, bureau and agency that lives by Federal appropriation.

And we are also going to enlist the help and ideas of many dedicated and hard-working Government employees at all levels who want a more efficient Government just as much as the rest of us do. I know that many of them are demoralized by the confusion and waste they confront in their work as a result of failed and failing policies.

Our instructions to the groups we enlist will be simple and direct. We will remind them that Government programs exist at the sufferance of the American taxpayer and are paid for with money earned by working men and women and programs that represent a waste of their money—a theft from their pocketbooks—must have that waste eliminated or that program must go. It must go by Executive Order where possible, by Congressional action where necessary.

Everything that can be run more effectively by state and local government we shall turn over to state and local government, along with the funding resources to pay for it. We are going to put an end to the money merry-go-round where our money becomes Washington's money, to be spent by states and cities exactly the way the Federal bureaucrats tell us it has to be spent.

I will not accept the excuse that the Federal Government has grown so big and powerful that it is beyond the control of any President, any administration or Congress. We are going to put an end to the notion that the American taxpayer exists to fund the Federal Government. The

Federal Government exists to serve the American people and to be accountable to the American people. On January 20, we are going to reestablish that truth.

Also on that date we are going to initiate action to get substantial relief for our taxpaying citizens and action to put people back to work. None of this will be based on any new form of monetary tinkering or fiscal sleight-of-hand. We will simply apply to government the common sense that we all use in our daily lives.

Work and family are at the center of our lives, the foundation of our dignity as a free people. When we deprive people of what they have earned, or take away their jobs, we destroy their dignity and undermine their families. We can't support families unless there are jobs; and we can't have jobs unless the people have both money to invest and the faith to invest it.

These are concepts that stem from an economic system that for more than 200 years has helped us master a continent, create a previously undreamed-of-prosperity for our people and has fed millions of others around the globe and that system will continue to serve us in the future if our Government will stop ignoring the basic values on which it was built and stop betraying the trust and good will of the American workers who keep it going.

The American people are carrying the heaviest peacetime tax burden in our nation's history—and it will grow even heavier, under present law, next January. We are taxing ourselves into economic exhaustion and stagnation, crushing our ability and incentive to save, invest and produce.

This must stop. We must halt this fiscal self-destruction and restore sanity to our economic system.

I've long advocated a 30 percent reduction in income tax rates over a period of three years. This phased tax reduction would begin with a 10 percent "down payment" tax cut in 1981, which the Republicans in Congress and I have already proposed.

A phased reduction of tax rates would go a long way toward easing the heavy burden on the American people. But we shouldn't stop there.

Within the context of economic conditions and appropriate budget priorities during each fiscal year of my Presidency, I would strive to go further. This would include improvement in business depreciation taxes so we can stimulate investment in order to get plants and equipment replaced, put more Americans back to work and put our nation back on the road to being competitive in world commerce. We will also work to reduce the cost of government as a percentage of our gross national product.

The first task of national leadership is to set realistic and honest priorities in our policies and our budget, and I pledge that my Administration will do that.

When I talk of tax cuts, I am reminded that every major tax cut in this century has strengthened the economy, generated renewed productivity and ended up yielding new revenues for the Government by creating new investment, new jobs and more commerce among our people.

The present Administration has been forced by us Republicans to play follow-the-leader with regard to a tax cut. But in this election year, we must take with the proverbial "grain of salt" any tax cut proposed by those who have already given us the greatest tax increase in our nation's history.

When those in leadership give us tax increases and tell us we must also do with less, have they thought about those who've always had less—especially the minorities? This is like telling them that just as they step on the first rung of the ladder of opportunity, the ladder is being pulled out from under them. That may be the Democratic leadership's message to the minorities, but it won't be our message. Ours will be: We have to move ahead, but we're not going to leave anyone behind.

Thanks to the economic policies of the Democratic Party, millions of Americans find themselves out of work. Millions more have never even had a fair chance to learn new skills, hold a decent job or secure for themselves and their families a share in the prosperity of this nation.

It's time to put America back to work, to make our cities and towns resound with the confident voices of men and women of all races, nationalities and faiths bringing home to their families a paycheck they can cash for honest money.

For those without skills, we'll find a way to help them get new skills.

For those without job opportunities, we'll stimulate new

opportunities, particularly in the inner cities where they live.

For those who've abandoned hope, we'll restore hope and we'll welcome them into a great national crusade to make America great again.

When we move from domestic affairs, and cast our eyes abroad, we see an equally sorry chapter in the record of the present Administration:

—A Soviet combat brigade trains in Cuba, just 90 miles from our shores.

—A Soviet army of invasion occupies Afghanistan, further threatening our vital interests in the Middle East.

—America's defense strength is at its lowest ebb in a generation, while the Soviet Union is vastly outspending us in both strategic and conventional arms.

—Our European allies, looking nervously at the growing menace from the East, turn to us for leadership and fail to find it.

—And incredibly, more than 50, as you've been told from this platform so eloquently already, more than 50 of our fellow Americans have been held captive for over eight months by a dictatorial power that holds us up to ridicule before the world.

Adversaries large and small test our will and seek to confound our resolve, but we are given weakness when we need strength; vacillation when the times demand firmness.

The Carter Administration lives in the world of make-believe. Every day, drawing up a response to that day's problems, troubles, regardless of what happened yesterday and what'll happen tomorrow.

But you and I live in a real world, where disasters are overtaking our nation without any real response from Washington.

This is make-believe, self-deceit, and above all, transparent hypocrisy.

For example, Mr. Carter says he supports the volunteer Army, but he lets military pay and benefits slip so low that many of our enlisted personnel are actually eligible for food stamps. Re-enlistment rates drop and, just recently, after he fought all week against a proposed pay increase for our men and women in the military, he then helicoptered out to our carrier the U.S.S. Nimitz, which was returning from long months of duty in the Indian Ocean, and told the crew of that ship that he advocated better pay for them and their comrades. Where does he really stand, now that he's back on shore?

Well, I'll tell you where I stand. I do not favor a peace-time draft or registration, but I do favor pay and benefit levels that will attract and keep highly motivated men and women in our volunteer forces and back them up with an active reserve trained and ready for instant call in case of emergency.

You know, there may be a sailor at the helm of the ship of state, but the ship has no rudder. Critical decisions are made at times almost in comic fashion, but who can laugh?

Who was not embarrassed when the Administration handed a major propaganda victory in the United Nations to the enemies of Israel, our staunch Middle East ally for three decades, and then claimed that the American vote was a "mistake," the result of a "failure of communication" between the President, his Secretary of State and his U.N. Ambassador?

Who does not feel a growing sense of unease as our allies, facing repeated instances of an amateurish and confused Administration, reluctantly conclude that America is unwilling or unable to fulfill its obligations as leader of the free world?

Who does not feel rising alarm when the question in any discussion of foreign policy is no longer, "Should we do something?" but "Do we have the capacity to do anything?"

The Administration which has brought us to this state is seeking your endorsement for four more years of weakness, indecision, mediocrity and incompetence. No. No. No American should vote until he or she has asked: Is the United States stronger and more respected now than it was three-and-a-half years ago? Is the world safer, a safer place in which to live?

It is the responsibility of the President of the United States, in working for peace, to insure that the safety of our people cannot successfully be threatened by a hostile foreign power. As President, fulfilling that responsibility will be my No. 1 priority.

We're not a warlike people. Quite the opposite. We always seek to live in peace. We resort to force infrequently and with great reluctance—and only after we've determined that it is absolutely necessary. We are awed—and rightly so—by the forces of destruction at loose in the world in this nuclear era.

But neither can we be naive or foolish. Four times in my lifetime America has gone to war, bleeding the lives of its young men into the sands of island beachheads, the fields of Europe and the jungles and rice paddies of Asia. We know only too well that war comes not when the forces of freedom are strong, it is when they are weak that tyrants are tempted.

We simply cannot learn these lessons the hard way again without risking our destruction.

Of all the objectives we seek, first and foremost is the establishment of lasting world peace. We must always stand ready to negotiate in good faith, ready to pursue any reasonable avenue that holds forth the promise of lessening tensions and furthering the prospects of peace. But let our friends and those who may wish us ill take note: The United States has an obligation to its citizens and to the people of the world never to let those who would destroy freedom dictate the future course of life on this planet. I would regard my election as proof that we have renewed our resolve to preserve world peace and freedom. That this nation will once again be strong enough to do that.

Now this evening marks the last step, save one, of a campaign that has taken Nancy and me from one end of this great nation to the other, over many months and thousands and thousands of miles. There are those who question the way we choose a President, who say that our process imposes difficult and exhausting burdens on those who seek the office. I have not found it so.

It is impossible to capture in words the splendor of this vast continent which God has created as our portion of His creation. There are no words to express the extraordinary strength and character of this breed of people we call Americans.

Everywhere we've met thousands of Democrats, Independents and Republicans from all economic conditions, walks of life bound together in that community of shared values of family, work, neighborhood, peace and freedom. They are concerned, yes, they're not frightened. They're disturbed, but not dismayed. They are the kind of men and women Tom Paine had in mind when he wrote, during the darkest days of the American Revolution, "We have it in our power to begin the world over again."

Nearly 150 years after Tom Paine wrote those words, an American President told the generation of the Great Depression that it had a "rendezvous with destiny." I believe this generation of Americans today also has a rendezvous with destiny.

Tonight, let us dedicate ourselves to renewing the American compact. I ask you not simply to "trust me," but to trust your values—our values—and to hold me responsible for living up to them. I ask you to trust that American spirit which knows no ethnic, religious, social, political, regional or economic boundaries; the spirit that burned with zeal in the hearts of millions of immigrants from every corner of the earth who came here in search of freedom.

Some say that spirit no longer exists. But I've seen it—I've felt it—all across the land, in the big cities, the small towns and in rural America. It's still there, ready to blaze into life if you and I are willing to do what has to be done; we have to do the practical things, the down-to-earth things, such as creating policies that will stimulate our economy, increase productivity and put America back to work.

The time is now to limit Federal spending; to insist on a stable monetary reform and to free ourselves from imported oil.

The time is now to resolve that the basis of a firm and principled foreign policy is one that takes the world as it is and seeks to change it by leadership and example; not by harangue, harassment or wishful thinking.

The time is now to say that we shall seek new friendships and expand others and improve others, but we shall not do so by breaking our word or casting aside old friends and allies.

And the time is now to redeem promises made to the American people by another candidate, in another time and another place. He said:

"For three years I have been going up and down this country preaching that government—Federal, state and local—costs too much. I shall not stop that preaching. As an immediate program of action, we must abolish useless offices. We must eliminate unnecessary functions of government.

"We must consolidate subdivisions of government and, like the private citizen, give up luxuries which we can no longer afford." And then he said:

"I propose to you my friends, and through you, that government of all kinds, big and little, be made solvent and that the example be set by the President of the United States and his Cabinet."

That was Franklin Delano Roosevelt's words as he accepted the Democratic nomination for President in 1932.

The time is now, my fellow Americans, to recapture our destiny, to take it into our own hands. And to do this it will take many of us, working together. I ask you tonight, all over this land, to volunteer your help in this cause so that we can carry our message throughout the land.

Isn't it time that we, the people, carry out these unkept promises? That we pledge to each other and to all America on this July day 48 years later, that we now intend to do just that?

I have thought of something that's not a part of my speech and worried over whether I should do it. Can we doubt that only a Divine Providence placed this land, this island of freedom, here as a refuge for all those people in the world who yearn to breathe free? Jews and Christians enduring persecution behind the Iron Curtain; the boat people of Southeast Asia, Cuba and of Haiti; the victims of drought and famine in Africa, the freedom fighters in Afghanistan, and our own countrymen held in savage captivity.

I'll confess that I've been a little afraid to suggest what I'm going to suggest. I'm more afraid not to. Can we begin our crusade joined together in a moment of silent prayer?

God bless America.

Thank you.

Inaugural Address

"Putting America Back to Work"

January 20, 1981, Washington, D.C.
by Ronald Reagan,
President of the United States

Thank you.

Senator Hatfield, Mr. Chief Justice, Mr. President, Vice President Bush, Vice President Mondale, Senator Baker, Speaker O'Neill, Reverend Moomaw, and my fellow citizens:

To a few of us here today, this is a solemn and most momentous occasion. And yet, in the history of our nation, it is a commonplace occurrence.

The orderly transfer of authority as called for in the Constitution routinely takes place as it has for almost two centuries and few of us stop to think how unique we really are.

In the eyes of many in the world, this every-four-year ceremony we accept as normal is nothing less than a miracle.

Mr. President, I want our fellow citizens to know how much you did to carry on this tradition.

By your gracious cooperation in the transition process you have shown a watching world that we are a united people pledged to maintaining a political system which guarantees individual liberty to a greater degree than any other. And I thank you and your people for all your help in maintaining the continuity that is the bulwark of our republic.

The business of our nation goes forward.

These United States are confronted with an economic affliction of great proportions.

We suffer from the longest and one of the worst sustained inflations in our national history. It distorts our economic decisions, penalizes thrift and crushes the struggling young and the fixed-income elderly alike. It threatens to shatter the lives of millions of our people.

Idle industries have cast workers into unemployment, human misery and personal indignity.

Those who do work are denied a fair return for their labor by a tax system which penalizes successful achievement and keeps us from maintaining full productivity.

But great as our tax burden is, it has not kept pace with public spending. For decades we have piled deficit upon deficit, mortgaging our future and our children's future for the temporary convenience of the present.

To continue this long trend is to guarantee tremendous social, cultural, political and economic upheavals.

You and I, as individuals, can, by borrowing, live beyond our means, but only for a limited period of time. Why then should we think that collectively, as a nation, we are not bound by that same limitation?

We must act today in order to preserve tomorrow. And let there be no misunderstanding—we're going to begin to act beginning today.

The economic ills we suffer have come upon us over several decades.

They will not go away in days, weeks or months, but they will go away. They will go away because we as Americans have the capacity now, as we have had in the past, to do whatever needs to be done to preserve this last and greatest bastion of freedom.

In this present crisis, government is not the solution to our problem; government is the problem.

From time to time, we've been tempted to believe that society has become too complex to be managed by self-rule, that government by an elite group is superior to government for, by and of the people.

But if no one among us is capable of governing himself, then who among us has the capacity to govern someone else?

All of us together—in and out of government—must bear the burden. The solutions we seek must be equitable with no one group singled out to pay a higher price.

We hear much of special interest groups. Well our concern must be for a special interest group that has been too long neglected.

It knows no sectional boundaries, or ethnic and racial divisions and it crosses political party lines. It is made up of men and women who raise our food, patrol our streets, man our mines and factories, teach our children, keep our homes and heal us when we're sick.

Professionals, industrialists, shopkeepers, clerks, cabbies and truck drivers. They are, in short, "We the people." This breed called Americans.

Well, this Administration's objective will be a healthy, vigorous, growing economy that provides equal opportunities for all Americans with no barriers born of bigotry or discrimination.

Putting America back to work means putting all Americans back to work. Ending inflation means freeing all Americans from the terror of runaway living costs.

All must share in the productive work of this "new beginning," and all must share in the bounty of a revived economy.

With the idealism and fair play which are the core of our system and our strength, we can have a strong prosperous America at peace with itself and the world.

So as we begin, let us take inventory.

We are a nation that has a government—not the other way around. And this makes us special among the nations of the earth.

Our Government has no power except that granted it by the people. It is time to check and reverse the growth of government which shows signs of having grown beyond the consent of the governed.

It is my intention to curb the size and influence of the Federal establishment and to demand recognition of the distinction between the powers granted to the Federal Government and those reserved to the states or to the people.

All of us need to be reminded that the Federal Government did not create the states; the states created the Federal Government.

Now, so there will be no misunderstanding, it's not my intention to do away with government.

It is rather to make it work—work with us, not over us; to stand by our side, not ride on our back. Government can and must provide opportunity, not smother it; foster productivity, not stifle it.

If we look to the answer as to why for so many years we achieved so much, prospered as no other people on earth, it was because here in this land we unleashed the energy and individual genius of man to a greater extent than has ever been done before.

Freedom and dignity of the individual have been more available here than in any other place on earth. The price for this freedom at times has been high, but we have never been unwilling to pay that price.

It is no coincidence that our present troubles parallel and are proportionate to the intervention and intrusion in our lives that result from unnecessary and excessive growth of Government.

It is time for us to realize that we are too great a nation to limit ourselves to small dreams. We're not, as some would have us believe, doomed to an inevitable decline. I do not believe in a fate that will fall on us no matter what we do. I do believe in a fate that will fall on us if we do nothing.

So, with all the creative energy at our command let us begin an era of national renewal. Let us renew our determination, our courage, and our strength. And let us renew our faith and our hope. We have every right to dream heroic dreams.

Those who say that we're in a time when there are no heroes—they just don't know where to look. You can see heroes every day going in and out of factory gates. Others, a handful in number, produce enough food to feed all of us and then the world beyond.

You meet heroes across a counter—and they're on both sides of that counter. There are entrepreneurs with faith in themselves and faith in an idea who create new jobs, new wealth and opportunity.

There are individuals and families whose taxes support the Government and whose voluntary gifts support church, charity, culture, art and education. Their patriotism is quiet but deep. Their values sustain our national life.

Now, I have used the words "they" and "their" in speaking of these heroes. I could say "you" and "your" because I'm addressing the heroes of whom I speak—you, the citizens of this blessed land.

Your dreams, your hopes, your goals are going to be the dreams, the hopes and the goals of this Administration, so help me God.

We shall reflect the compassion that is so much a part of your makeup.

How can we love our country and not love our countrymen? And loving them reach out a hand when they fall, heal them when they're sick and provide opportunity to make them self-sufficient so they will be equal in fact and not just in theory?

Can we solve the problems confronting us? Well the answer is an unequivocal and emphatic yes.

To paraphrase Winston Churchill, I did not take the oath I've just taken with the intention of presiding over the dissolution of the world's strongest economy.

In the days ahead I will propose removing the roadblocks that have slowed our economy and reduced productivity.

Steps will be taken aimed at restoring the balance between the various levels of government. Progress may be slow—measured in inches and feet, not miles—but we will progress.

It is time to reawaken this industrial giant, to get government back within its means and to lighten our punitive tax burden.

And these will be our first priorities and on these principles there will be no compromise.

On the eve of our struggle for independence, a man who might've been one of the greatest among the Founding Fathers, Dr. Joseph Warren, president of the Massachusetts Congress, said to his fellow Americans, "Our country is in danger, but not to be despaired of. On you depend the fortunes of America. You are to decide the important question upon which rest the happiness and the liberty of millions yet unborn. Act worthy of yourselves."

Well I believe we the Americans of today are ready to act worthy of ourselves, ready to do what must be done to insure happiness and liberty for ourselves, our children and our children's children.

As we renew ourselves here in our own land, we will be seen as having greater strength throughout the world. We will again be the exemplar of freedom and a beacon of hope for those who do not now have freedom.

To those neighbors and allies who share our freedom, we will strengthen our historic ties and assure them of our support and firm commitment.

We will match loyalty with loyalty. We will strive for mutually beneficial relations. We will not use our friendship to impose on their sovereignty, for our own sovereignty is not for sale.

As for the enemies of freedom, those who are potential adversaries, they will be reminded that peace is the highest aspiration of the American people. We will negotiate for it, sacrifice for it; we will not surrender for it—now or ever.

Our forbearance should never be misunderstood. Our reluctance for conflict should not be misjudged as a failure of will.

When action is required to preserve our national security, we will act. We will maintain sufficient strength to prevail if need be, knowing that if we do we have the best chance of never having to use that strength.

Above all we must realize that no arsenal or no weapon in the arsenals of the world is so formidable as the will and moral courage of free men and women.

It is a weapon our adversaries in today's world do not have.

It is a weapon that we as Americans do have.

Let that be understood by those who practice terrorism and prey upon their neighbors.

I am told that tens of thousands of prayer meetings are being held on this day; for that I am deeply grateful. We are a nation under God, and I believe God intended for us to be free. It would be fitting and good, I think, if on each inaugural day in future years it should be declared a day of prayer.

This is the first time in our history that this ceremony has been held, as you've been told, on this West Front of the Capitol.

Standing here, one faces a magnificent vista, opening up on this city's special beauty and history.

At the end of this open mall are those shrines to the giants on whose shoulders we stand.

Directly in front of me, the monument to a monumental man, George Washington, father of our country. A man of humility who came to greatness reluctantly. He led America out of revolutionary victory into infant nationhood.

Off to one side, the stately memorial to Thomas Jefferson. The Declaration of Independence flames with his eloquence.

And then beyond the Reflecting Pool, the dignified columns of the Lincoln Memorial. Whoever would understand in his heart the meaning of America will find it in the life of Abraham Lincoln.

Beyond those monuments, monuments to heroism is the Potomac River, and on the far shore the sloping hills of Arlington National Cemetery with its row upon row of simple white markers bearing crosses or Stars of David. They add up to only a tiny fraction of the price that has been paid for our freedom.

Each of those markers is a monument to the kind of hero I spoke of earlier.

Their lives ended in places called Belleau Wood, the Argonne, Omaha Beach, Salerno and halfway around the world on Guadalcanal, Tarawa, Pork Chop Hill, the Chosin Reservoir, and in a hundred rice paddies and jungles of a place called Vietnam.

Under such a marker lies a young man, Martin Treptow, who left his job in a small town barber shop in 1917 to go to France with the famed Rainbow Division.

There, on the Western front, he was killed trying to carry a message between battalions under heavy artillery fire.

We are told that on his body was found a diary.

On the flyleaf under the heading, "My Pledge," he had written these words:

"America must win this war. Therefore I will work, I will save, I will sacrifice, I will endure, I will fight cheerfully and do my utmost, as if the issue of the whole struggle depended on me alone."

The crisis we are facing today does not require of us the kind of sacrifice that Martin Treptow and so many thousands of others were called upon to make.

It does require, however, our best effort, and our willingness to believe in ourselves and to believe in our capacity to perform great deeds; to believe that together with God's help we can and will resolve the problems which now confront us.

And after all, why shouldn't we believe that? We are Americans.

God bless you and thank you. Thank you very much.

State of the Union
Delivered to the American People
January 25, 1983

This solemn occasion marks the 196th time that a President of the United States has reported on the State of the Union since George Washington did so in 1790. That is a lot of reports, but there is no shortage of new things to say about the state of the Union. The very key to our success has been our ability, foremost among nations, to preserve our lasting values by making change work for us rather than against us.

I would like to talk with you this evening about what we can do together—not as Republicans and Democrats, but as Americans—to make tomorrow's America happy and prosperous at home, strong and respected abroad and at peace in the world.

As we gather here tonight, the state of our Union is strong but, our economy is troubled. For too many of our fellow citizens—farmers, steel and auto workers, lumbermen, black teenagers, and working mothers—this is a painful period. We must do everything in our power to bring their ordeal to an end. It has fallen to us, in our time, to undo damage that was a long time in the making, and to begin the hard but necessary task of building a better future for ourselves and our children.

We have a long way to go, but thanks to the courage, patience and strength of our people, America is on the mend.

Let me give you just one important reason why I believe this—and it involves many members of this body.

Just 10 days ago, after months of debate and deadlock, the bipartisan Commission on Social Security accomplished the seemingly impossible.

Social Security, as some of us had warned for so long, faced disaster. I, myself, have been speaking about this problem for almost 30 years. As 1983 began, the system stood on the brink of bankruptcy, a double victim of our economic ills. First, a decade of rampant inflation drained its reserves as we tried to protect beneficiaries from the spiraling cost of living. Then the recession and the sudden end of inflation withered the expanding wage base and increasing revenues the system needs to support the 36 million Americans who depend on it.

When the Speaker of the House, the Senate majority leader and I formed the bipartisan Commission on Social Security, pundits and experts predicted that party divisions and conflicting interests would prevent the Commission from agreeing on a plan to save Social Security.

Well, sometimes, even here in Washington, the cynics are wrong. Through compromise and cooperation, the members of the commission overcame their differences and achieved a fair, workable plan. They proved that, when it comes to the national welfare, Americans can still pull together for the common good.

Tonight, I am especially pleased to join with the Speaker and the Senate majority leader in urging the Congress to enact this plan within the next hundred days.

There are elements in it, of course, that none of us prefers, but taken together it forms a package all of us can support. It asks for some sacrifice by all—the self-employed, beneficiaries, workers, new Government employees, and the better-off among the retired—but it imposes an undue burden on none. And, in supporting it, we keep an important pledge to the American people: the integrity of the Social Security system will be preserved—and no one's payments will be reduced.

The commission's plan will do the job. Indeed, it must do the job. We owe it to today's older Americans—and today's younger workers.

So, before we go any further, I ask you to join with me in saluting the members of the commission who are here tonight, and Senate Majority Leader Howard Baker and Speaker Tip O'Neill, for a job well done.

I hope and pray the bipartisan spirit that guided you in this endeavor will inspire all of us as we face the challenges of the year ahead.

Nearly half a century ago, in this chamber, another American President, Franklin Delano Roosevelt, in his second State of the Union Message, urged America to look to the future—to meet the challenge of change and the need for leadership that looks forward, not backward.

"Throughout the world," he said, "change is the order of the day. In every nation economic problems long in the making have brought crises of many kinds for which the masters of old practice and theory were unprepared."

He also reminded us that "the future lies with those wise political leaders who realize that the great public is interested more in Government than in politics."

So, let us, in these next two years—men and women of both parties and every political shade—concentrate on the long-range, bipartisan responsibilities of Government, not the short-term temptations of partisan politics.

The problems we inherited were far worse than most inside and out of Government has expected; the recession was deeper that most inside and out of Government had predicted. Curing those problems has taken more time, and a higher toll, than any of us wanted. Unemployment is far too high. Projected Federal spending—if Government refuses to tighten its own belt—will also be far too high and could weaken and shorten the economic recovery now underway.

This recovery will bring with it a revival of economic confidence and spending for consumer items and capital goods—the stimulus we need to restart our stalled economic engines. The American people have already stepped up their rate of saving, assuring that the funds needed to modernize our factories and improve our technology will once again flow to business and industry.

The inflationary expectations that led to a 21 ½ percent prime rate and soaring mortgage rates two years ago are now reduced by almost half. Lenders have started to realize that double-digit inflation is no longer a way of life. So, interest rates have tumbled, paving the way for recovery in vital industries like housing and autos.

The early evidence of that recovery has started coming in. Housing starts for the fourth quarter of 1982 were up 45 percent from a year ago. And housing permits—a sure indicator of future growth—were up a whopping 60 percent.

We are witnessing an upsurge of productivity and impressive evidence that American industry will once again become competitive in markets at home and abroad—in-

suring more jobs and better incomes for the nation's work
force.

But our confidence must also be tempered by realism
and patience. Quick fixes and artificial stimulants, repeat-
edly applied over decades, are what brought on the inflationary disorders that we have now paid such a heavy
price to cure.

The permanent recovery in employment, production
and investment we seek will not come in a sharp, short
spurt. It will build carefully and steadily in the months
and years ahead.

In the meantime, the challenge of Government is to
identify the things we can do now to ease this massive
economic transition for the American people.

The Federal budget is both a symptom and a cause of our
economic problems. Unless we reduce the dangerous
growth rate in Government spending, we could face the
prospect of sluggish economic growth into the indefinite
future. Failure to cope with this problem now could mean
as much as a trillion dollars more in national debt in the
next four years alone. That would average $4,300 in addi-
tional debt for every man, woman, and child in our nation.

To assure a sustained recovery, we must continue getting runaway spending under control to bring those deficits down. If we do not, the recovery will be too short,
unemployment will remain too high, and we will leave an
unconscionable burden of national debt for our children.
That we must not do.

Let us be clear about where the deficit problem comes
from. Contrary to the drumbeat we have been hearing for
the last few months, the deficits we face are not rooted in
defense spending. Taken as a percentage of the gross national product, our defense spending happens to be only
about four-fifths of what it was in 1970. Nor is the deficit,
as some would have it, rooted in tax cuts. Even with our
tax cuts, taxes as a fraction of gross national product remain about the same as they were in 1970.

The fact is, our deficits come from the uncontrolled
growth of the budget for domestic spending. During the
1970's, the share of our national income devoted to this
domestic spending increased by more than 60 percent—
from 10 cents out of every dollar produced by the American people to 16 cents. In spite of all our economics and

efficiencies, and without adding any new programs, basic, necessary domestic spending provided for in this year's budget will grow to almost $1 trillion over the next five years.

The deficit problem is a clear and present danger to the basic health of our Republic. We need a plan to overcome this danger—a plan based on these principles:

It must be bipartisan. Conquering the deficits and putting the Government's house in order will require the best efforts of all of us.

It must be fair. Just as all will share in the benefits that will come from recovery, all would share fairly in the burden of transition.

It must be prudent. The strength of our national defense must be restored so that we can pursue prosperity in peace and freedom while maintaining our commitment to the truly needy.

Finally, it must be realistic. We cannot rely on hope alone.

With these guiding principles in mind, let me outline a four-part plan to increase economic growth and reduce deficits.

First, in my Budget Message, I will recommend a Federal spending freeze. I know this is strong medicine, but so far we have only cut the rate of increase in Federal spending. The Government has continued to spend more money each year, though not as much more as it did in the past. Taken as a whole, the budget I am proposing for the next fiscal year will increase no more than the rate of inflation —in other words, the Federal Government will hold the line on real spending. That is far less than many American families have had to do in these difficult times.

I will request that the proposed six-month freeze in cost-of-living adjustments recommended by the bipartisan Social Security Commission be applied to other Government-related retirement programs. I will also propose a one-year-freeze on a broad range of domestic spending programs, and for Federal civilian and military pay and pension programs.

Second, I will ask the Congress to adopt specific measures to control the growth of the so-called "uncontrollable" spending programs. These are the automatic spending programs, such as food stamps, that cannot be simply frozen—and that have grown by over 400 percent since 1970. They are the largest single cause of the built-in or "structural" deficit problem. Our standard here will be fairness—insuring that the taxpayers' hard-earned dollars go only to the truly needy; that none of them are turned away; but that fraud and waste are stamped out. And, I am sorry to say, there is a lot of it out there. In the food stamp program alone, last year we identified almost $1.1 billion in overpayments. The taxpayers are not the only victims of this kind of abuse; the truly needy suffer as funds intended for them are taken by the greedy. For everyone's sake, we must put an end to such waste and corruption.

Third, I will adjust our program to restore America's defense by proposing $55 billion in defense savings over the next five years. These are savings recommended to me by the Secretary of Defense, who has assured me they can be safely achieved and will not diminish our ability to negotiate arms reductions or endanger America's security. We will not gamble with our national survival.

Fourth, because we must insure reduction and eventual elimination of deficits over the next several years, I will propose a stand-by tax limited to no more than 1 percent of the gross national product to start in fiscal 1986. It would last no more than three years and would start only if the Congress has first approved our spending freeze and budget control program. You could say that this is an insurance policy for the future—a remedy that will be at hand if needed, but only resorted to if absolutely necessary.

In the meantime, we will continue to study ways to simplify the tax code and make it more fair for all Americans. This is a goal that every American who has ever struggled with a tax form can understand.

At the same time, however, I will oppose any efforts to undo the basic tax reforms we have already enacted—including the 10 percent tax break coming to taxpayers this July and the tax indexing which will protect all Americans from inflationary bracket creep in the years ahead.

I realize that this four-part plan is easier to describe than it will be to enact. But the looming deficits that hang over us—and over America's future—must be reduced.

The path I have outlined is fair, balanced, and realistic. If enacted, it will insure a steady decline in deficits, aiming toward a balanced budget by the end of the decade. It is the only path that will lead to a strong, sustained recovery.

Let us follow that path together.

No domestic challenge is more crucial than providing stable, permanent jobs for all Americans who want to work. The recovery will provide jobs for most but others will need special help and training for new skills. Shortly, I will submit to the Congress the Employment Act of 1983 designed to get at the special problems of the long-term unemployed as well as young people trying to enter the job market. I will propose extending unemployment benefits, including special incentives to employers who hire the long-term unemployed, providing programs for displaced workers, and helping federally funded and state-administered unemployment insurance programs provide workers with training and relocation assistance. Finally, our proposal will include new incentives for summer youth employment to help young people get a start in the job market.

We must offer both short-term help and long-term hope for our unemployed. I hope we can work together on this, as we did last year in enacting the landmark Job Training Partnership Act. Regulatory reform legislation, a responsible clean air act and passage of Enterprise Zone legislation will also create new incentives for jobs and opportunity.

One out of every five jobs in our country depends on trade. So, I will propose a broader strategy in the field of international trade—one that increases the openness of our trading system and is fairer to America's farmers and workers in the world marketplace. We must have adequate export financing to sell American products overseas. I will ask for new negotiating authority to remove barriers and get more of our products into foreign markets. We must strengthen the organization of our trade agencies and make changes in our domestic laws and international trade policy to promote free trade and the increased flow of American goods, services and investments.

Our trade position can also be improved by making our port system more efficient. Better, more active harbors translate into stable jobs in our coal fields, railroads, trucking industry and ports. After two years of debate, it is time for us to get together and enact a port modernization bill.

Education, training and retraining are fundamental to our success as are research, development and productivity. Labor, management and government at all levels can and must participate in improving these tools of growth. Tax policy, regulatory practices and Government programs all need constant re-evaluation in terms of our competitiveness. Every American has a role, and a stake, in international trade.

We Americans are still the world's technological leader in most fields. We must keep that edge, and to do so we need to begin renewing the basics—starting with our educational system. While we grew complacent, others have acted. Japan, with a population only about half the size of ours, graduates from its universities more engineers than we do. If a child does not receive adequate math and science teaching by the age of 16, he or she has lost the chance to be a scientist or engineer.

We must join together—parents, teachers, grassroots groups, organized labor and the business community—to revitalize American education by setting a standard of excellence.

In 1983, we seek four major education goals:

—A quality education initiative to encourage a substantial upgrading of math and science instruction through block grants to the states.

—Establishment of education savings accounts that will give middle- and lower-income families an incentive to save for their children's college education and, at the same time, encourage a real increase in savings for economic growth.

—Passage of tuition tax credits for parents who want to send their children to private or religiously affiliated schools.

—A constitutional amendment to permit voluntary school prayer; God never should have been expelled from America's classrooms.

Our commitment to fairness means that we must assure legal and economic equality for women, and eliminate, once and for all, all traces of unjust discrimination against women from the U.S. Code. We will not tolerate wage discrimination based on sex and we intend to strengthen enforcement of child support laws to insure that single parents, most of whom are women, do not suffer unfair financial hardship. We will also take action to remedy inequities in pensions. These initiatives will be joined by others to continue our efforts to promote equity for women.

Also in the area of fairness and equity, we will ask for extension of the Civil Rights Commission, which is due to expire this year. The Commission is an important part of the ongoing struggle for justice in America, and we strongly support its reauthorization. Effective enforcement of our nation's fair housing laws is also essential to insuring equal opportunity. In the year ahead, we will work to strengthen enforcement of fair housing laws for all Americans.

The time has also come for major reform of our criminal justice statutes and acceleration of the drive against organized crime and drug trafficking. It is high time we make our cities safe again. This Administration hereby declares all-out war on big-time organized crime and the drug racketeers who are poisoning our young people. We will also implement recommendations of our Task Force on Victims of Crime, which will report to me this week.

American agriculture, the envy of the world, has become the victim of its own success. With one farmer now producing enough food to feed himself and 77 other people, America is confronted with record surplus crops and commodity prices below the cost of production. We must strive, through innovation like the payment-in-kind "crop swap" approach, and an aggressive export policy, to restore health and vitality to rural America. Meanwhile, I have instructed the Department of Agriculture to work individually with farmers with debt problems to help them through these tough times.

Over the past year, our Task Force on Private Sector Initiatives has successfully forged a working partnership involving leaders of business, labor, education and Government to address the training needs of American workers. Thanks to the task force, private sector initiatives are now under way in all 50 states of the Union and thousands of working people have been helped in making the shift from dead-end jobs and low-demand skills to the growth areas of high technology and the service economy. Additionally, a major effort will be focused on encouraging the expansion of private community child care. The new advisory council on private sector initiatives will carry on and extend this vital work of encouraging private initiative in 1983.

In the coming year we will also act to improve the quality of life for Americans by curbing the skyrocketing cost of health care that is becoming an unbearable financial burden for so many. And we will submit legislation to provide catastrophic illness insurance coverage for older Americans.

I will also shortly submit a comprehensive federalism proposal that will continue our efforts to restore to states and local governments their roles as dynamic laboratories of change in a creative democracy.

During the next several weeks, I will send to the Congress a series of detailed proposals on these and other topics and look forward to working with you on the development of these initiatives.

So far, I have concentrated mainly on the problems posed by the future. But in almost every home and workplace in America, we are already witnessing reason for great hope—the first flowering of the man-made miracles of high technology, a field pioneered and still led by our country.

To many of us now, computers, silicon chips, data processing, cybernetics and all the other innovations of the dawning high technology age are as mystifying as the workings of the combustion engine must have been when the first Model T rattled down Main Street U.S.A.

But, as surely as America's pioneer spirit made us the industrial giant of the 20th century, the same pioneer spirit today is opening up another vast frontier of opportunity—the frontier of high technology. In conquering this frontier, we cannot write off our traditional industries, but we must develop the skills and industries that will make us a pioneer of tomorrow. This Administration is committed to keeping America the technological leader of the world now and into the 21st century.

Let us turn briefly to the international arena. America's leadership role in the world came to us because of our own strength and because of the values which guide us as a society: free elections, a free press, freedom of religious choice, free trade unions, and, above all, freedom for the individual and rejection of the arbitrary power of the State. These values are the bedrock of our strength. They unite us in a stewardship of peace and freedom with our allies and friends in NATO, in Asia, in Latin America and elsewhere. They are also the values which in the recent past some among us had begun to doubt and view with a cynical eye.

Fortunately, we and our allies have rediscovered the strength of our common democratic values. And we are applying them as the cornerstone of a comprehensive strategy for peace with freedom. In London last year, I announced the commitment of the United States to developing an infrastructure of democracy throughout the world. We intend to pursue this democratic initiative vigorously. The future belongs not to governments and ideologies which oppress their peoples but to democratic systems of self-government which encourage individual initiative and guarantee personal freedom.

But our strategy for peace with freedom must also be based on strength—economic strength and military strength. A strong American economy is essential to the well-being and security of our friends and allies. The restoration of a strong, healthy American economy has been and remains one of the central pillars of our foreign policy. The progress I have been able to report to you tonight, will, I know, be as warmly welcomed by the rest of the free world as it is by the American people.

We must also recognize that our own economic well-being is inextricably linked to the world economy. We export over 20 percent of our industrial production, and 40 percent of our farmland products for export. We will continue to work closely with the industrialized democracies of Europe and Japan and with the International Monetary Fund to ensure it has adequate resources to help bring the world economy back to strong, noninflationary growth. As the leader of the West and as a country that has become great and rich because of economic freedom, America must be an unrelenting advocate of free trade. As some nations are tempted to turn to protectionism, our strategy cannot be to follow them but to lead the way toward freer trade. To this end, in May of this year, America will host an Economic Summit meeting in Williamsburg, Virginia.

As we begin our third year, we have put in place a defense program that redeems the neglect of the past decade. We have developed a realistic military strategy to deter threats to the peace, and to protect our freedom if deterrence fails. Our armed forces are finally properly paid, after years of neglect, are well-trained, and becoming better equipped and supplied—and the American uniform is once more worn with pride. Most of the major systems needed for modernizing our defenses are already underway and we will be addressing one key system—the MX missile—in consultations with Congress in a few months.

America's foreign policy is once again based on bipartisanship—on realism, strength, full partnership and consultation with our allies, and constructive negotiation with potential adversaries. From the Middle East to southern Africa to Geneva, American diplomats are taking the initiative to make peace and lower arms levels. We should be proud of our role as peacemakers.

In the Middle East last year, the United States played the major role in ending the tragic fighting in Lebanon, and negotiating the withdrawal of the P.L.O. from Beirut.

Last September, I outlined principles to carry on the peace process begun so promisingly at Camp David. All the people of the Middle East should know that, in the year ahead, we will not flag in our efforts to build on that foundation to bring them the blessings of peace.

In Central America and the Caribbean Basin, we are likewise engaged in a partnership for peace, prosperity and democracy. Final passage of the remaining portions of our Caribbean Basin Initiative, which passed the House last year, is one of this Administration's top legislative priorities for 1983.

The security and economic assistance policies of this Administration in Latin America and elsewhere, are based on realism and represent a critical investment in the future of the human race. This undertaking is a joint responsibility of the executive and legislative branches, and I am counting on the cooperation and statesmanship of the Congress to help us meet this essential foreign policy goal.

At the heart of our strategy for peace is our relationship with the Soviet Union.

The past year saw a change in Soviet leadership. We are

prepared for a positive change in Soviet-American relations. But the Soviet Union must show, by deeds as well as words, a sincere commitment to respect the rights and sovereignty of the family of nations. Responsible members of the world community do not threaten or invade their neighbors and they restrain their allies from aggression.

For our part, we are vigorously pursuing arms reductions negotiations with the Soviet Union. Supported by our allies, we have put forward draft agreements proposing significant weapons reductions to equal and verifiable lower levels. We insist on an equal balance of forces. And, given the overwhelming evidence of Soviet violations of international treaties concerning chemical and biological weapons, we also insist that any agreement we sign can and will be verifiable.

In the case of intermediate-range nuclear forces, we have proposed the complete elimination of the entire class of land-based missiles. We are also prepared to carefully explore serious Soviet proposals. At the same time, let me emphasize that allied steadfastness remains a key to achieving arms reductions.

With firmness and dedication, we will continue to negotiate. Deep down, the Soviets must know it is in their interest as well as ours to prevent a wasteful arms race. And once they recognize our unshakeable resolve to maintain adequate deterrence, they will have every reason to join us in the search for greater security and arms reductions. When that moment comes—and I am confident that it will—we will have taken an important step toward a more peaceful future for all of the world's people.

A very wise man, Bernard Baruch, once said that America has never forgotten the nobler things that brought her into being and that light her path. Our country is a special place because we Americans have always been sustained, through good times and bad, by a noble vision—a vision not only of what the world around us is today, but of what we, as a free people, can make it tomorrow.

We are realists; we solve our problems instead of ignoring them, no matter how loud the chorus of despair around us.

But we are also idealists, for it was an ideal that brought our ancestors to these shores from every corner of the world.

Right now we need both realism and idealism. Millions of our neighbors are without work. It is up to us to see that they are not without hope. This is a task for all of us. And may I say Americans have rallied to this cause proving once again that we are the most generous people on Earth.

We who are in Government must take the lead in restoring the economy. The single thing that can start the wheels of industry turning again is further reduction of interest rates. Another one or two points can mean tens of thousands of jobs. Right now, with inflation as low as it is, 3.9 percent, there is room for interest rates to come down.

Only fear prevents their reduction. A lender, as we know, must charge an interest rate that recovers the depreciated value of the dollars loaned. That depreciation is, of course, the amount of inflation. Today, interest rates are based on the fear that Government will resort to measures, as it has in the past, that will send inflation zooming again.

We who serve here in this capital must erase that fear by making it absolutely clear that we will not stop fighting inflation; that together we will do only those things that will lead to lasting economic growth.

Yes, the problems confronting us are large and forbidding. And, certainly, no one can or should minimize the plight of millions of our friends and neighbors who are living in the bleak emptiness of unemployment. But we must and can give them good reason to be hopeful.

Back over the years, citizens like ourselves have gathered within these walls when our nation was threatened; sometimes when its very existence was at stake. Always, with courage and common sense, they met the crises of their time and lived to see a stronger, better and more prosperous country.

The present situation is no worse and in fact not as bad as some of those they faced. Time and again, they proved that there is nothing we Americans cannot achieve as free men and women.

Yes, we still have problems—plenty of them. But it is just plain wrong—unjust to our country and unjust to our people—to let those problems stand in the way of the most important truth of all: America is on the mend.

We owe it to the unfortunate to be aware of their plight and to help them in every way we can. No one can quarrel with that—we must and do have compassion for all the victims of this economic crisis. But the big story about America today is the way that millions of confident, caring people—those extraordinary "ordinary" Americans who never make the headlines and will never be interviewed—are laying the foundation, not just for recovery from our present problems, but for a better tomorrow for all our people.

From coast to coast, on the job and in classrooms and laboratories, at new construction sites and in churches and community groups, neighbors are helping neighbors. And they've already begun the building, the research, the work and the giving that will make our country great again.

I believe this because I believe in them—in the strength of their hearts and minds, in the commitment each of them brings in their daily lives, be they high or humble. The challenge for us in Government is to be worthy of them—to make Government a help, not a hindrance to our people in the challenging but promising days ahead.

If we do that, if we care what our children and our children's children will say of us, if we want them one day to be thankful for what we did here in these temples of freedom, we will work together to make America better for our having been here—not just in this year, or in this decade, but in the next century and beyond.

Address to the American People
On Lebanon and Grenada
October 27, 1983, Washington, D.C.

My fellow Americans, some two months ago we were shocked by the brutal massacre of 269 men, women and children, in the shooting down of a Korean airliner. Now, in these past several days, violence has erupted again, in Lebanon and Grenada.

In Lebanon, we have some 1,600 marines, part of a multinational force that's trying to help the people of Lebanon restore order and stability to that troubled land. Our marines are assigned to the south of the city of Beirut near the only airport operating in Lebanon. Just a mile or so to the north is the Italian contingent and not far from them the French and a company of British soldiers.

This past Sunday, at 22 minutes after 6, Beirut time, with dawn just breaking, a truck looking like a lot of other vehicles in the city approached the airport on a busy main road. There was nothing in its appearance to suggest it was any different than the trucks or cars that were normally seen on and around the airport. But this one was different.

At the wheel was a young man on a suicide mission. The truck carried some 2,000 pounds of explosives, but there was no way our marine guards could know this. Their first warning that something was wrong came when the truck crashed through a series of barriers, including a chain link fence and barbed wire entanglements. The guards opened fire but it was too late.

The truck smashed through the doors of the headquarters building in which our marines were sleeping and instantly exploded. The four-story building collapsed in a pile of rubble.

More than 200 of the sleeping men were killed in that one hideous insane attack. Many others suffered injury and are hospitalized here or in Europe. This was not the end of the horror.

At almost the same instant another vehicle on a suicide and murder mission crashed into the headquarters of the French peacekeeping force, an eight-story building, destroying and killing more than 50 French soldiers.

Prior to this day of horror there had been several tragedies for our men in the multinational force; attacks by snipers and mortar fire had taken their toll. I call the bereaved parents and/or widows of the victims to express on behalf of all of us our sorrow and sympathy. Sometimes there were questions. And now many of you are asking: Why should our young men be dying in Lebanon? Why is Lebanon important to us?

Well, it's true Lebanon is a small country more than five and a half thousand miles from our shores, on the edge of what we call the Middle East. But every President who has occupied this office in recent years has recognized that peace in the Middle East is of vital concern to our nation and, indeed, to our allies in Western Europe and Japan. We've been concerned because the Middle East is a powder keg. Four times in the last 30 years, the Arabs and Israelis have gone to war and each time the world has teetered near the edge of catastrophe. The area is key to the economic and political life of the West. Its strategic importance, its energy resources, the Suez Canal, the well-being of the nearly 200 million people living there; all are vital to us and to world peace.

If that key should fall into the hands of a power or powers hostile to the free world, there would be a direct threat to the United States and to our allies.

We have another reason to be involved. Since 1948, our nation has recognized and accepted a moral obligation to assure the continued existence of Israel as a nation. Israel shares our democratic values and is a formidable force an invader would have to reckon with. For several years, Lebanon has been torn by internal strife. Once a prosperous, peaceful nation, its Government had become ineffective in controlling the militias that warred on each other.

Sixteen months ago, we were watching on our TV screens the shelling and bombing of Beirut, which was being used as a fortress by P.L.O. bands. Hundreds and hundreds of civilians were being killed and wounded in the daily battles. Syria, which makes no secret of its claim that Lebanon should be part of a greater Syria, was occupying a large part of Lebanon. Today, Syria has become a home for 7,000 Soviet advisers and technicians who man a massive amount of Soviet weaponry, including SS-21 ground-to-ground missiles capable of reaching vital areas of Israel.

A little over a year ago, hoping to build on the Camp David accords, which have led to peace between Israel and Egypt, I proposed a peace plan for the Middle East to end the wars between the Arab states and Israel. It was based on U.N. Resolutions 242 and 338 and called for a fair and just solution to the Palestinian problem, as well as a fair and just settlement of issues between the Arab states and Israel.

Before the necessary negotiations could begin, it was essential to get all foreign forces out of Lebanon and to end the fighting there. So why are we there? Well, the answer is straightforward: to help bring peace to Lebanon and stability to the vital Middle East. To that end the multinational force was created to help stabilize the situation in Lebanon until a government could be established and the Lebanese Army mobilized to restore Lebanese sovereignty over its own soil as the foreign forces withdrew.

Israel agreed to withdraw as did Syria. But Syria then reneged on its promise. Over 10,000 Palestinians who had been bringing ruin down on Beirut, however, did leave the country. Lebanon has formed a Government under the leadership of President Gemayel and that Government, with our assistance and training, has set up its own army. In only a year's time that army has been rebuilt. It's a good army composed of Lebanese and all factions.

A few weeks ago the Israeli Army pulled back to the Awali River in southern Lebanon. Despite fierce resistance by Syrian-backed forces the Lebanese Army was able to hold the lines and maintain the defensive perimeter around Beirut. In the year that our marines have been there Lebanon has made important steps toward stability and order. The physical presence of the marines lends support to both the Lebanese Government and its army. It allows the hard work of diplomacy to go forward. Indeed without the peacekeepers from the U.S., France, Italy and Britain, the efforts to find a peaceful solution in Lebanon would collapse.

As for that narrower question, what exactly is the operational mission of the marines, the answer is to secure a piece of Beirut; to keep order in their sector and to prevent the area from becoming a battlefield. Our Marines are not just sitting in an airport. Part of their task is to guard that airport. Because of their presence, the airport has remained operational. In addition they patrol the surrounding area. This is their part—a limited but essential part—in a larger effort that I described.

If our marines must be there, I'm asked, why can't we make them safer? Who committed this latest atrocity against them and why? Well, we'll do everything we can to insure that our men are as safe as possible. We ordered the battleship New Jersey to join our naval forces offshore. Without even firing them, the threat of its 16-inch guns silenced those who once fired down on our marines from the hills. And they're a good part of the reason we've suddenly had a cease-fire. We're doing our best to make our forces less vulnerable to those who want to snipe at them or send in future suicide missions.

Secretary Schultz called me today from Europe, where he was meeting with the foreign ministers of our allies and the multinational force. They remain committed to our task, and plans were made to share information as to how we can improve security for all our men.

We have strong circumstantial evidence that the attack on our marines was directed by terrorists who used the same method to destroy our embassy in Beirut. Those who directed this atrocity must be dealt justice, and they will be. The obvious purpose behind the sniping and now this attack was to weaken the American will and force the withdrawal of U.S. and French forces from Lebanon.

The clear intent of the terrorists was to limit our support of the Lebanese Government and to destroy the ability of the Lebanese people to determine their own destiny. To answer those who ask if we're serving any purpose in being there, let me answer a question with a question: would the terrorists have launched their suicide attacks against the multinational force if it were not doing its job?

The multinational force was attacked precisely because it is doing the job it was sent to do in Beirut. It is accomplishing its mission.

Now then, where do we go from here?

What can we do to help Lebanon gain greater stability

so that our marines can come home? I believe we can take three steps now that will make a difference.

First, we will accelerate the search for peace and stability in that region. Little attention is being paid to the fact that we have had special envoys there working literally around the clock to bring the warring factions together. This coming Monday in Geneva, President Gemayel of Lebanon will sit down with other factions from his country to see if national reconciliation can be achieved. He has our firm support.

I will soon be announcing a replacement for Bud McFarlane who was preceded by Phil Habib. Both worked tirelessly and must be credited for much, if not most, of the progress we've made.

Second, we'll work even more closely with our allies in providing support for the Government of Lebanon and for the rebuilding of a national consensus.

Third, we will insure that the multinational peacekeeping forces, our Marines, are given the greatest possible protection. Our Commandant of the Marine Corps, General Kelley, returned from Lebanon today and will be advising us on steps we can take to improve security.

Vice President Bush returned just last night from Beirut and gave me a full report on his brief visit.

Beyond our progress in Lebanon let us remember that our main goal and purpose is to achieve a broader peace in all of the Middle East. The factions and bitterness that we see in Lebanon are just a microcosm of the difficulties that are spread across much of that region. A peace initiative for the entire Middle East, consistent with the Camp David accord, and U.N. Resolutions 242 and 338, still offers the best hope for bringing peace to the region.

Let me ask those who say we should get out of Lebanon: If we were to leave Lebanon now, what message would that send to those who foment instability and terrorism? If America were to walk away from Lebanon, what chance would there be for a negotiated settlement producing the unified, democratic Lebanon? If we turned our backs on Lebanon now, what would be the future of Israel? At stake is the fate of only the second Arab country to negotiate a major agreement with Israel. That's another accomplishment of the past year, the May 17 accord signed by Lebanon and Israel.

If terrorism and intimidation succeed, it'll be a devastating blow to the peace process and to Israel's search for genuine security. It won't be just Lebanon sentenced to a future of chaos. Can the United States, or the free world, for that matter, stand by and see the Middle East incorporated into the Soviet bloc? What of Western Europe and Japan's dependence on Middle East oil for the energy to fuel their industries? The Middle East is, as I said, vital to our national security and economic well-being.

Brave young men have been taken from us. Many others have been grievously wounded. Are we to tell them their sacrifice was wasted when they gave their lives in defense of our national security as much as any man who ever died fighting in a war?

We must not strip every ounce of meaning and purpose from their courageous sacrifice. We are a nation with global responsibilities, we're not somewhere else in the world protecting someone else's interest. We're there protecting our own.

I received a message from the father of a marine in Lebanon. He told me: "In a world where we speak of human rights, there is a sad lack of acceptance of responsibility. My son has chosen the acceptance of responsibility for the privilege of living in this country."

Certainly in this country one does not inherently have rights unless the responsibility for these rights is accepted.

Dr. Kenneth Morrison said that while he was waiting to learn if his son was one of the dead. I was thrilled for him, to learn today that his son, Ross, is alive and well and carrying on his duties in Lebanon.

Let us meet our responsibilities. For longer than any of us can remember, the people of the Middle East have lived from war to war with no prospect for any other future. That dreadful cycle must be broken.

Why are we there? When a Lebanese mother told one of our ambassadors that her little girl had only attended school two of the last eight years. Now, because of our presence there, she said her daughter could live a normal life. With patience and firmness, we can help bring peace to that strife-torn region and make our own lives more secure.

Our role is to help the Lebanese put their country together, not to do it for them.

Now I know another part of the world is very much on our minds. A place much closer to our shores. Grenada. The island is only twice the size of the District of Columbia with a total population of about 110,000 people. Grenada and a half-dozen other Caribbean islands here were, until recently, British colonies. They are now independent states and members of the British Commonwealth.

While they respect each other's independence they also feel a kinship with each other and think of themselves as one people. In 1979 trouble came to Grenada. Maurice Bishop, a protégé of Fidel Castro, staged a military coup and overthrew the government which had been elected under the constitution left to the people by the British.

He sought the help of Cuba in building an airport, which he claimed was for tourist trade, but which looked suspiciously suitable for military aircraft, including Soviet-built long-range bombers. The six sovereign countries and one remaining colony are joined together in what they call the Organization of Eastern Caribbean States. The six became increasingly alarmed as Bishop built an army greater than all of their combined.

Obviously, it was not purely for defense. In this last year or so, Prime Minister Bishop gave indications that he might like better relations with the United States. He even made a trip to our country and met with senior officials at the White House and the State Department. Whether he was serious or not, we'll never know.

On October 12, a small group in his militia seized him and put him under arrest. They were, if anything, even more radical and devoted to Castro's Cuba than he had been. Several days later, a crowd of citizens appeared before Bishop's home, freed him and escorted him toward the headquarters of the Military Council. They were fired upon. A number, including some children, were killed and Bishop was seized. He and several members of his Cabinet were subsequently executed and a 24-hour shoot-to-kill curfew was put in effect. Grenada was without a government, its only authority exercised by a self-proclaimed band of military men.

There were then about 1,000 of our citizens on Grenada, 800 of them students in St. George's University Medical School. Concern that they'd be harmed or held as hostages, I ordered a flotilla of ships then on its way to Lebanon with

Marines—part of our regular rotation program—to circle
south on a course that would put them somewhere in the
vicinity of Grenada in case there should be a need to evacu-
ate our people.

Last weekend I was awakened in the early morning
hours and told that six members of the Organization of
Eastern Caribbean States joined by Jamaica and Barbados
had sent an urgent request that we join them in a military
operation to restore order and democracy to Grenada.

They were proposing this action under the terms of a
treaty, a mutual assistance pact that existed among them.
These small peaceful nations needed our help. Three of
them don't have armies at all and the others have very
limited forces.

The legitimacy of their request plus my own concern for
our citizens dictated my decision. I believe our Government has a responsibility to go to the aid of its citizens if
their right to life and liberty is threatened. The nightmare
of our hostages in Iran must never be repeated.

We knew we had little time and that complete secrecy
was vital to insure both the safety of the young men who
would undertake this mission and the Americans they
were about to rescue.

The joint chiefs worked around the clock to come up
with a plan. They had little intelligence information about
conditions on the island. We had to assume that several
hundred Cubans working on the airport could be military
reserves. As it turned out the number was much larger
and they were a military force. Six hundred of them have
been taken prisoner and we have discovered a complete
base with weapons and communications equipment which
makes it clear a Cuban occupation of the island had been
planned.

Two hours ago we released the first photos from Grenada. They included pictures of a warehouse of military
equipment, one of three we've uncovered so far. This warehouse contained weapons and ammunition stacked almost
to the ceiling, enough to supply thousands of terrorists.

Grenada, we were told, was a friendly island paradise
for tourism. Well it wasn't. It was a Soviet-Cuban colony
being readied as a major military bastion to export terror
and undermine democracy.

We got there just in time.

I can't say enough in praise of our military. Army Rangers and paratroopers, Navy Marine and Air Force personnel, those who planned a brilliant campaign and those who carried it out.

Almost instantly our military seized the two airports, secured the campus where most of our students were and they're now in the mopping-up phase.

It should be noted that in all the planning, a top priority was to minimize risk, to avoid casualties to our own men and also the Grenadian forces as much as humanly possible. But there were casualties. And we all owe a debt to those who lost their lives or were wounded. They were few in number but even one is a tragic price to pay.

It's our intention to get our men out as soon as possible.

Prime Minister Eugenia Charles of Dominica—I called that wrong, she pronounces it Dom-in-EE-kuh—she is chairman of O.E.C.S. She's calling for help from Commonwealth nations in giving the people their right to establish a constitutional government on Grenada. We anticipate that the Governor General, a Grenadian, will participate in setting up a provisional government in the interim.

The events in Lebanon and Grenada, though oceans apart, are closely related. Not only has Moscow assisted and encouraged the violence in both countries, but it provides direct support through a network of surrogates and terrorists. It is no coincidence that when the thugs tried to wrest control of Grenada, there were 30 Soviet advisers and hundreds of military and paramilitary forces on the island. At the moment of our landing we communicated with the governments of Cuba and the Soviet Union and told them we would offer shelter and security to their people on Grenada. Regrettably, Castro ordered his men to fight to the death and some did. The others will be sent to their homelands.

Now there was a time when our national security was based on a standing army here within our own borders and shore batteries of artillery along our coast, and of course a navy to keep the sea lanes open for the shipping of things necessary to our well-being. The world has changed. Today our national security can be threatened in far-away places. It's up to all of us to be aware of the strategic importance of such places and to be able to identify them.

Sam Rayburn once said that freedom is not something

a nation can work for once and win forever. He said it's like an insurance policy; its premiums must be kept up to date. In order to keep it we have to keep working for it and sacrificing for it just as long as we live. If we do not, our children may not know the pleasure of working to keep it for it may not be theirs to keep.

In these last few days, I've been more sure than I've ever been that we Americans of today will keep freedom and maintain peace. I've been made to feel that by the magnificent spirit of our young men and women in uniform, and by something here in our nation's capital.

In this city, where political strife is so much a part of our lives, I've seen Democratic leadership in the Congress join their Republican colleagues, send a message to the world that we're all Americans before we're anything else, and when our country is threatened, we stand shoulder to shoulder in support of men and women in the armed forces.

May I share with you something I think you'd like to know? It's something that happened to the Commandant of our Marine Corps, General Paul Kelley, while he was visiting our critically injured marines in an Air Force hospital. It says more than any of us could ever hope to say about the gallantry and heroism of these young men, young men who served so willingly so that others might have a chance at peace and freedom in their own lives and in the life of their country.

I'll let General Kelley's words describe the incident. He spoke of a "young marine with more tubes going in and out of his body than I have ever seen in one body. He couldn't see very well. He reached up and grabbed my four stars just to make sure I was who I said I was. He held my hand with a firm grip. He was making signals and we realized he wanted to tell me something. We put a pad of paper in his hand and he wrote: 'semper fi.'"

Well, if you've been a marine, or if, like myself, you're an admirer of the Marines, you know those words are a battle cry, a greeting and a legend in the Marine Corps. They're Marine shorthand for the motto of the Corps: Semper Fidelis, Always Faithful.

General Kelley has a reputation for being a very sophisticated general and a very tough marine, but he cried when he saw those words, and who can blame him. That marine, and all those others like him living and dead, have been faithful to their ideals. They've given willingly of themselves so that a nearly defenseless people in a region of great strategic importance to the free world will have a chance someday to live lives free of murder and mayhem and terrorism. I think that young marine and all of his comrades have given every one of us something to live up to.

They were not afraid to stand up for their country or no matter how difficult and slow the journey might be, to give to others that last best hope of a better future.

We cannot and will not dishonor them now and the sacrifices they made by failing to remain as faithful to the cause of freedom and the pursuit of peace as they have been.

I will not ask you to pray for the dead because they are safe in God's loving arms and beyond the need of our prayers.

I would like to ask you all, wherever you may be in this blessed land, to pray for these wounded young men, and to pray for the bereaved families of those who gave their lives for our freedom.

God bless you and God bless America.